PIERS
OF KENT

PIERS
OF KENT

MARTIN EASDOWN

TEMPUS

Frontispiece: Cockleshell Beach, 1920s.

First published 2007

Tempus Publishing Limited
The Mill, Brimscombe Port,
Stroud, Gloucestershire, GL5 2QG
www.tempus-publishing.com

British Library Cataloguing in Publication Data.
A catalogue record for this book is available from the British Library.

ISBN 978 0 7524 4220 4

Typesetting and origination by Tempus Publishing Limited.
Printed in Great Britain.

CONTENTS

ACKNOWLEDGEMENTS

The libraries at Dartford, Gravesend, Sheerness, Herne Bay, Margate, Ramsgate Deal, Dover and Folkestone
National Archives, Kew
East Kent Archives, Whitfield
Medway Archive Centre, Strood
Kent County Archives, Maidstone
The National Piers Society
Herne Bay Records Society
Mike Still, Assistant Museum Manager, Dartford Borough Museum
Kenneth Chamberlain
Alan Boakes
Linda Sage
Eamonn Rooney
Alan F. Taylor
Peter & Annie Bamford
Terry Wheeler
Michael Child
Bob Hollingsbee
Alan Brigham
Susan Lees

INTRODUCTION

With its long coastline and comparatively mild climate, it was no surprise that the County of Kent was at the forefront of the growth of the British seaside resort. Margate was one of the earliest of the country's watering places and was advertising sea bathing as early as 1736. Then just a small fishing village, the town grew rapidly following Richard Russell's dissertation in 1750 on the benefits of drinking and bathing in seawater. Margate was helped in this respect by its comparative closeness to London, which was just seventy-two miles away. Nearby, Ramsgate also began to flourish, as did Gravesend, where Rosherville Gardens was a great day trip attraction for Londoners.

In the days before nationwide rail travel and a good road system, the majority of people travelled to resorts by hoys and, later, steamers. However, for those towns without good harbours, there was a problem getting passengers ashore. A leaky rowing boat or the back of some sturdy local fishermen originally had to suffice, but in 1813-14, Ryde, on the Isle of Wight erected a landing stage for the safe handling of visitors and the idea of a pier was born. The famous Chain Pier at Brighton was erected in 1822-23, and within a short time had acquired the status as the most fashionable promenade in town.

Margate's harbour was unsuitable as a landing place except at high tide, so in 1824 the Jarvis Landing Stage was erected. Herne Bay was a purposely created resort of the early steamboat era where a long pier was erected in 1832 to feed off the thriving London-Margate traffic. The resorts Gravesend (1834-35), Sheerness (1835) and Deal (1838) also erected early landing piers, but towns with good harbours, Ramsgate and the burgeoning resorts of Dover and Folkestone, did without piers.

Folkestone was Kent's premier example of a seaside resort where rapid growth could be attributed to the coming of the railway. Following its arrival in 1843, the local landowner, the Earl of Radnor, laid out the elegant West End of the town with its grand crescents, squares and avenues fronting onto the famous cliff-top Leas Promenade. The intended clientele was to be strictly upper class and Lord Radnor's policemen ensured that the trippers did not soil the exclusivity of the Leas.

Margate was connected to the South Eastern Railway in 1846 and its fierce rival the London, Chatham & Dover Railway in 1863. The resort's initial aspirations to be a select watering place was swamped by hoards of working-class trippers arriving on the steamers and trains, but it managed to maintain a 'posh end' at Cliftonville. Ramsgate, once the favoured retreat of Coleridge, also became popular with trippers. It was left to neighbouring Broadstairs to carve itself out a niche as the more select end of Thanet. Kent's middle-ranking resorts included Herne Bay, Deal, Sheerness, Whitstable (and its satellite Tankerton), Dover, Sandgate, Hythe and Westgate-on-Sea; the latter trying to outdo even Folkestone for exclusivity. One of Kent's earliest resorts, Gravesend, had virtually ceased to be a watering place by 1900 due to the pollution of the Thames and decline of Rosherville Gardens.

The county's early piers had largely proved to be failures. The wooden piers at Herne Bay and Deal had quickly succumbed to the twin horrors of storm damage and marine worms, while the Jarvis Landing Stage at Margate, which often trapped its customers on the pier head at high tide, was wrecked by a storm in 1851. In contrast, the cast-iron piers at Gravesend (admittedly situated in more sheltered water) had proved more durable and Margate's replacement structure became the first full-scale pier in the country to be constructed of cast iron. Although known as the 'Jetty' (to distinguish it from the stone harbour pier) this was a full-fledged seaside pier, and in 1864 Deal followed suit with a handsome iron structure. It was found that people actually enjoyed just walking up and down a pier and relished a stroll over the waves without the discomfort of feeling seasick; and what's more they would pay a toll for the privilege.

From the 1860s a 'mania' developed amongst resorts to erect a showpiece pleasure pier. In Kent, following Margate (1855) and Deal (1864), Herne Bay erected an iron pier in 1873 (greatly extended between 1896-99), followed by Ramsgate (1881), Folkestone (1888) and Dover (1893). Even little Pegwell Bay (1879) and Tankerton (1894) managed to have small piers for a time, yet proposed piers in resorts such as Broadstairs, Westgate, Hythe and Littlestone never saw the light of day. However by 1910, when the pier-building era came to an end, almost one hundred pleasure piers had sprouted around the coast of Britain. To cater for ever-increasing forms of entertainment, piers were adapted to house ornate wooden pavilions, floral halls, theatres and amusements, such as roller skating, divers, camera obscura and mutoscopes.

In addition to its pleasure piers, Kent also had plenty of other piled pier structures of interest, including the railway/steamer piers of the Thames and Medway, which are covered in less significant detail in this book. The solid concrete/stone harbour and landing piers at Margate, Ramsgate, Dover and Folkestone however are not included, but Dover's Prince of Wales Pier (which boasted some nice ironwork for many years) and Broadstairs' interesting wooden harbour pier are briefly featured.

With the majority of Kent's seaside piers now only distant memories (only Deal's post-war concrete pier and a stub of Herne Bay survive, but Gravesend's Town and Royal Terrace and some of the Medway piers are also still extant), this book will hopefully serve as a reminder of the county's golden pier age.

Martin Easdown, *2007*

1

RIVER THAMES PIERS

ERITH

During the 1840s Erith was a day trip destination for Londoners, and on 22 August 1842 a 444ft wooden pier was opened by the Guardians of the Wheatley Estate. The opening day was celebrated with various events, including rowing matches, duck hunting and a jingling match, which involved men hitting each other with ash sticks until the last one standing was the winner. Previous attempts to build a pier by local shopkeeper Jonathan Monk in 1840 and a group of Woolwich businessmen had both been unsuccessful.

The *Diamond* and *Star*, travelling between London and Gravesend, called at the pier daily. The Pier Hotel was added in 1844 and on 6 July 1845 an 8-acre pleasure garden designed by Andrew McClure was opened. The gardens featured a conservatory, refreshment rooms, arboretum, bowling green, archery field, grand walk, maze and fountain.

However the opening of the railway to Erith in 1849 reduced the amount of calls at the pier and the popularity of the town as a resort fell in face of competition from Margate and Southend. The tourist trade was virtually killed off by the opening in 1865 of the Southern Outfall Works at Crossness, which disgorged tons of sewage into the river daily. In 1874 the pier and gardens were sold by the Wheatley Estate and were eventually put to industrial use; firstly by coal merchants Beadle Bros and then in 1896 by Wm Cory & Sons Ltd. In the 1890s a second pier was built upstream which extended outwards beyond the original structure before extending downstream to join it.

The wooden piers survived until 1957 when they were replaced by an extensive concrete pier that could accommodate larger ships. The Pier Hotel was demolished and replaced by warehouses. These were closed in the early 1990s and Morrisons was opened on the site in 1999. Fortunately the pier was retained for public use and today it is a well-maintained promenade giving excellent views of the shipping in the river.

DARTFORD LONG REACH

A small pier (more strictly a floating pontoon) was constructed at Long Reach by the Metropolitan Asylums Board (MAB) in 1883 to receive smallpox patients. The MAB had just acquired 8.25 acres of land at Long Reach (adjoining their hospital ships in the Thames) and Gore Farm, Darenth, where it was intended to erect shore-based smallpox hospitals. The Southern Hospital was erected at Gore Farm and housed smallpox patients until 1903, whilst the Long Reach Hospital was opened on 27 February 1902. Two further hospitals, Orchard (1902) and Joyce Green (1903) were opened close to Long Reach. All three hospitals were connected by a horse-drawn tramway that ran to the pier.

The original wooden pier at Erith built in 1842 to catch steamer trade between London and Gravesend. The Pier Hotel was opened in 1845, but later replaced by warehouses. *Kenneth Chamberlain*

The present-day concrete pier at Erith opened in 1957. Once used for industrial purposes, it is now a fine promenade for both townsfolk and visitors. *Marlinova Collection*

The smallpox hospital ships lie off the Long Reach Pier at Dartford, *c.*1900. *KCC Libraries*

The pier basically consisted of an enclosed walkway leading to a floating pontoon. The angle of the walkway was heightened and lowered by the ebb and flow of the tide, whilst on the pontoon was a shed-like building placed between the timbers that supported the rise and fall of the pontoon.

The structure continued to be used until 1930 when the River Ambulance Service ceased following damage to the vessels *Lower Dolphin* and *Albert Victor* by a steamer at South Wharf on 24 July 1930. The pier remained in situ for a few more years, but had gone by the end of the 1930s. The tramway, which had been motor operated since 1924, remained in use as an internal link between the hospitals until closure in 1936.

By the 1970s, with the eradication of smallpox, all the river hospitals had closed bar Joyce Green, which had grown into a general hospital. However, with the opening of the new Darent Valley Hospital on 11 September 2000, Joyce Green was closed.

GREENHITHE

Like Erith, Greenhithe was a popular day resort for Londoners, being within each reach of the capital. On 19 April 1842, the Greenhithe Pier Company was formed at the Admiral Keppel Inn (later the Pier Hotel) with a capital of £2,000 in 400 shares of £5, with a deposit of £1 per share. The engineer engaged to erect the pier was a 'Mr Birch', which leads us to believe this was probably the partnership of John Brannis and Eugenius Birch. Eugenius went on to become the pier-builder supreme and Greenhithe was probably the first structure that he was involved in. The brothers designed an attractive 350ft pier, which became a port of call for the Gravesend-bound steamers.

In 1847, Summer Excursions in the County of Kent along the Banks of the Thames and Medway commented:

The appearance of Greenhithe from the river is eminently picturesque. Its red brick cottages and tall white cliffs project boldly forward from the dark woods of Swanscombe, which, stretching far away inland, bound the distant horizon. The pier is in much the same fashion as that at Erith. The village may claim precedence for cleanliness, and the neighbouring country is not a whit less beautiful and interesting. We are not, in fact, familiar with any spot within distance of the Metropolis, and so easily approachable, where a quiet holiday could be more agreeably spent than amidst its rural and sylvan scenes.

A rare photograph of the short-lived pier at Greenhithe, an elegant structure that bears a resemblance to the famous Chain Pier at Brighton. In the background can be seen one of the naval training ships based on the Thames. *Marlinova Collection*

The deep water pier at Northfleet was utilised almost exclusively for industrial use. *Marlinova Collection*

An early engraving of Rosherville Pier, *c*.1840. Also seen is the Rosherville Hotel, built in 1835 but demolished in 1970. *KCC Libraries*

Rosherville Pier in its later guise with a bridge leading to the floating pontoon, *c*.1890. *KCC Libraries*

The pier may have been the departure point on 10 May 1845 for Sir John Franklin's ill-fated voyage to find the north-west passage, while on 11 August 1863 Queen Victoria boarded the Royal Yacht *Victoria and Albert* from the pier amid the eager applause of a large gathering of young and old.

Sadly, with the decline of Greenhithe as a resort, the pier was demolished in 1875 and replaced by a causeway, which is partly still in place today. However, the pier is commemorated by the Pier Hotel (which nevertheless features the causeway on its sign) and Pier Road, which are situated amongst an interesting collection of old riverside buildings that give a flavour of the village's grand past.

NORTHFLEET

A deep-water wooden pier, used, as far as it is known, purely for industrial use.

ROSHERVILLE

In 1838 the Rosherville Pier Company was formed to erect a pier to serve the newly opened Rosherville Gardens; a favourite day trip destination for Londoners. In 1851 the pier was said to be moveable and ingeniously contrived to form a safe and pleasant landing place at all times of the tide.

Originally consisting of a wooden pier leading to a floating pontoon, the structure was later rebuilt to house a bridge that connected the pier to the pontoon. In 1910 the pier was refurbished for the City Steamboat Co. Ltd, yet by this time Rosherville Gardens had largely closed and the heyday of steamer traffic to the area was over.

The pier was subsequently demolished, but the entrance gates, which house a plaque commemorating the pier, and remains of the steps that led down to the pier can still be seen.

2

GRAVESEND TOWN PIER

The world's oldest surviving cast-iron pier and a Grade II listed structure, there was a landing place at the site of the Town Pier since at least Norman times.

In 1829, Gravesend Corporation erected the Town Quay and levied a penny for its use, but the landing stairs soon became inadequate to deal with the rising number of visitors to the, then fashionable, resort of Gravesend.

A Bill to sanction a pier in 1832 was defeated, but a resolution was passed by the corporation to erect a temporary pier. A Mr McIntosh was engaged to erect the structure, but on 22 June 1833 it was badly damaged by the local watermen who had fiercely opposed its construction[1]. The pier was repaired and 290,000 passengers were carried in 1833 to and from the town. The watermen were placated with compensation for the loss of income and the Town Quay Act received the Royal Assent for the building of a permanent pier next to the quay.

The noted engineer William Tierney Clark (1783-1852) was engaged as the engineer for the project. He had acquired his skills in cast iron when employed as a mechanic at the Coalbrookdale Ironworks and at John Rennie's Albion Ironworks at Blackfriars. Amongst Tierney Clark's other works was the completion of the Thames & Medway Canal and the Budapest Suspension Bridge. William Woods was appointed as contractor at a cost of £8,700, and whilst the pier was under construction the river traffic was transferred to the West Street jetty. By January 1834, the first 134ft of the pier had been completed, and on 27 January it was officially opened with great ceremony by Earl Darnley, which was followed by a grand banquet for 300 guests.

Work continued on the remainder of the pier, and by July 1834 it had been completed to 157ft x 40ft. The structure comprised three 40ft graceful flat iron arches, supported on twenty-six iron columns 18ft long x 2ft 9in in diameter. The pier head measured 76ft x 30ft and sported two attractive pavilions surmounted by decorative turrets; one housing a clock and the other a bell. A lighthouse was provided at the outer end to guide ships at night, and steps led down to the river providing access to vessels at all conditions of the tide.

In 1838 a new service was operated from the pier to Hungerford by the recently formed Eagle Steam Packet Company. In addition to its use as a landing stage, the pier was a fashionable promenade and during the summer, bands played on the pier head. However, in the mid-1840s the decision was taken to cover the pier, using supports for the roof from the original iron posts that held the handrails and lighting columns.

The builder who erected the pier, William Woods, had never been fully paid for his work, and in 1849 the corporation's chattels, including the mace, the councillor's robes and furniture at the Town Hall and on the Town Pier were seized by the Sheriff's officer following an action brought by Woods. He and some of the other creditor's were later paid and the chattels were recovered.

In 1851 the corporation obtained a ninety-nine-year lease, at a cost of £50 per annum, to operate the ferry from the pier. The operation, which used a tug that transported passengers, livestock and goods, was then put to tender. Unfortunately, principally due to the coming of the railway to Gravesend in 1849 and the subsequent loss of passengers, the corporation found itself bankrupt in 1852 and the Town Pier passed into receivership.

A view of the original open-decked Town Pier at Gravesend, pictured in 1833. In the following year it was replaced by the permanent cast-iron pier, which survives as the world's oldest cast-iron pier. *Marlinova Collection*

An Edwardian postcard published by Photocrom, showing one of the LTS Tilbury Ferry steamers at the landing stage. *Marlinova Collection*

Gravesend Town Pier in the hands of the London, Midland & Scottish Railway in the 1920s, suitably bearing the appearance of a railway station. The postcard was published by Thornton Bros of Gillingham. *Marlinova Collection*

A side view of Gravesend
Town Pier with the river at
high tide, *c.*1907. *Marlinova
Collection*

Gravesend Town Pier in
1975, looking rather down-
at-heel. *Marlinova Collection*

A 1975 photograph
showing the entrances to
the Town Pier Restaurant
and Cocktail Bar. *Marlinova
Collection*

A July 2003 photograph of Gravesend Town Pier following its restoration by Gravesham Council. Note the fine arched under-deck ironwork. *Marlinova Collection*

Gravesend Town Pier visitors in March 2006 with the addition of the Riva restaurant and bar. *Marlinova Collection*

The Tilbury Ferry landing stage at Gravesend, photographed in July 2003. Tilbury can clearly be seen on the opposite bank of the River Thames. *Marlinova Collection*

Gravesend West Street Pier was opened in 1886 at the termination of the London, Chatham & Dover Railway's line from Fawkham Junction. From 1916-39 the Batavia Shipping Line ran a service to Rotterdam from the pier. The branch was closed in 1968. The pier is now used for boat maintenance and seen here in July 2003. *Marlinova Collection*

Salvation for the corporation occurred in the form of the London, Tilbury & Southend Extension Railway. In 1852 they received authorisation to build the line, which included a clause to run a steam ferry between Tilbury and Gravesend, but compensation was to be paid to both Gravesend Corporation and the Board of Ordnance for their rights. The railway was opened two years later. The ferry crossing proved to be immediately popular with people from London's East End, who travelled down to Tilbury by train and then used the ferry crossing to Gravesend. The corporation's financial difficulties led them to lease their whole interest in the ferry, including those relating to the Board of Ordnance, to the LTSR for twenty-four years from 18 February 1856 at a cost of £750 per annum.

A pontoon was added to the pier in 1865 to allow two vessels to dock at the same time and fifteen years later, in 1880, the railway company acquired the corporation's interests in the ferries, on condition of still using the Town Pier where a 1d toll was still in operation. The company, which felt that the toll harmed their goods traffic, transferred all their traffic, except passengers, to the West Street Pier. However, in 1884 the LTSR purchased the pier from the receivers for £8,600, and so at last had full control of the ferry service and both landing places either side of the river. They added a 'railway touch' to the pier entrance by erecting a valanced-edge canopy. Increased passenger numbers enabled ferry prices to be reduced in 1888 from 4d to 2d single and 6d to 3d return.

The LTS was taken over by the Midland Railway on 1 July 1912, who in turn was absorbed into the LMS on 1 June 1923 following the Railway Amalgamation Act of 1922. British Railways took over upon Nationalisation in 1948, but in 1965 the ferry was transferred from the Town Pier to West Street Pier. A full list of the Tilbury ferries that had used the Town Pier from 1854-1965 were: PS *Earl of Leicester* (1854-77), PS *Earl of Essex* (1859-1906), PS *Tilbury* (1855-1905, renamed *Sir Walter Raleigh* in 1880), PS *Cato* (1876-94), PS *Thames* (1882-1913), PS *Tilbury* (1883-1922), TSS *Carlotta* (1893-1927), TSS *Rose* (1901-61), TSS *Catherine* (1903-61), TSS *Gertrude* (1906-32), TSS *Edith* (1911-61), MV *Catherine* (1960-65), MV *Edith* (1960-65) and MV *Rose* (1960-65).

From 1979, Sealink ran the Tilbury ferries, followed by Sea Containers (1984) and Stena Line (1990), but then Kent and Essex County Councils refused to subsidise the service, which was now down to just one ferry. White Horse Ferries took over the operation in 1991 and in the following year introduced a catamaran called *Great Expectations*. In 1996 this was replaced by the smaller vessel *Martin Chuzzlewit*, which now operates from a floating pontoon adjacent to the town pier.

As for the town pier itself, in 1969 an amusement arcade was opened as part of a plan to include dancing and a catering centre, and in 1978 the MV *Balmoral* sailed from the pier with trips to Clacton and Ramsgate. The Grade II listing was gained in 1984, the year the pier was sold to tug and barge owners C. Crawley Ltd for £75,000. In 1992 plans by White Horse Ferries to convert the pier into a major leisure complex were approved by Gravesham Borough Council. The following year saw a new river taxi service launched by the company from the pier to Canary Wharf, but this was soon discontinued.

In 1996 the pier was put up for sale, and two years later a repair notice was served to the owner by the council with the total cost of renovation estimated at over £1 million. Eventually in June 2000, the council itself purchased the pier at a cost of £70,000. They announced plans to restore the structure and add shops, a covered promenade and restaurant with grant assistance from English Heritage, the Heritage Lottery Fund, South East Development Agency (SEEDA), Kent County Council and the Manifold Trust. The design was prepared by quantity surveyors McBains Cooper and the work carried out by Mowlem Marine of Northfleet. The restoration work to the main structure had been completed by 2004, and during that summer the open deck of the pier was opened to the public as it awaited its commercial development. In early 2006 the Riva bar opened at the shore end of the pier.

GRAVESEND ROYAL TERRACE PIER

The Royal Terrace Pier began life as a 200ft wooden pier erected in 1835, but this was replaced in 1842 by a new iron pier erected by Fox Henderson to a design by John Baldry Redman at a cost of £9,200. The replacement pier was 250ft x 30ft and rested on twenty-two cast-iron columns. In common with the Town Pier, the length of the pier was covered by a wrought-iron roof which was ornamented with a Doric frieze below the windows. A lighthouse was situated on the pier head and a bridge led to a pontoon for steamer traffic. During the summer, bands performed on the pier and balls were held in the evenings.

In 1840 the Blackwall Railway Company operated three craft from the pier, but in 1851 the Diamond Company withdrew their steamers from the pier until the corporation reduced pier tolls from a penny to three farthings.

The pier's royal prefix was gained through its usage by the Royal Family. In 1858 the Princess Royal and her husband Crown Prince Frederick of Prussia sailed for Germany from the pier immediately following their marriage whilst fifty-eight local young ladies strewed flowers in their path. Princess Alexandra also arrived at the pier to marry the Prince of Wales in 1863[2].

A rather idealised early view of the Royal Terrace Pier at Gravesend; it appears amongst a town of classical proportions! *Marlinova Collection*

A rather more realistic view of the Royal Terrace Pier, showing the entrance buildings in the early years of the twentieth century. *Marlinova Collection*

A postcard scene of the Royal Terrace Pier published by Photocrom, *c.* 1910. The ironwork on this pier compares less favourably to that of the Town Pier. *Marlinova Collection*

Right: A photograph of Gravesend Royal Terrace Pier in 1975, taken from the landing stage bridge. By this time the pier was in use as a pilot station. *Marlinova Collection*

Below: Gravesend Royal Terrace Pier, photographed in September 2001. *Marlinova Collection*

The entrance to the Royal Terrace Pier in September 2001; little altered from a hundred years ago, although the same cannot be said for its surroundings. *Marlinova Collection*

A look along the covered deck of Gravesend Royal Terrace Pier in September 2001. *Marlinova Collection*

A PLA vessel moored at the Royal Terrace Pier in July 2003. *Marlinova Collection*

However in 1892, the pier was declared unsafe and closed, but it was restored two years later after £12,000 had been raised through public subscription. The Royal Terrace Pier Company subsequently extended the pier a further 100ft in 1895 and provided a new floating landing stage. Twelve years later, the pier was the scene of tragedy when the SS *T.E. Forster* sank after a collision with the SS *J.M. Smith* and the captain was drowned.

A Grade II listed structure, the pier is now privately owned by the Port of London River Authority, who in 1978 restored it at a cost of £333,000. Two years earlier, a figure of Poseidon, the God of the Sea, designed by Sean Price, was added outside the entrance of the pier. Water jets and night floodlighting today assist to animate the figure. In April 1977 the HMS *Cygnet* was moored at the pier for the official adoption ceremony with the Borough of Gravesham.

Notes

1 This event is commemorated by a mosaic mural commissioned by IMPACT, and designed by Kenneth and Oliver Budd in 1989 to be displayed on the previously bland brickwork of the Thames flood prevention barrier.
2 Over 100 years later in 1968, the Duke of Edinburgh and Prince Charles came ashore to the pier to visit the Thames Navigation Centre.

3

RIVER MEDWAY PIERS

PORT VICTORIA

This 561ft wooden pier was opened by the South Eastern Railway on 11 September 1882 as the terminus of its branch from Hoo Junction. Situated at the end of the isolated Hoo Peninsula and Isle of Grain, the railway ran to the end of the pier to connect a ferry service to Sheerness. The pier's isolation also led it to be used by European royalty, including Queen Victoria, as a favoured landing place close to London.

The line had been built by the SER to counter the rival service provided by its fierce rival the London, Chatham & Dover Railway from Queenborough Pier, which had opened in 1876. According to the SER, the opening of Queenborough Pier had violated the Continental Trade Agreement between the two companies to share all receipts from the Kent coast and continental traffic.

A wooden hotel was built adjoining the pier and in 1890 the Royal Corinthian Yacht Club was placed nearby. However, no further development took place and because of its seclusion Port Victoria was used by the Royal Yacht *Victoria and Albert*. The German Kaiser also used the pier, and in 1904 he helped contribute towards the restoration of Grain church, along with King Edward VII and Queen Alexandra. The last Royal Yacht tied up there in 1911, and three years later the Royal Corinthian Yacht Club moved to Burnham-on-Crouch.

Following a fire at Queenborough Pier in 1900, the Flushing service was transferred to Port Victoria until 1904, but the ferry service to Sheerness largely ceased in 1901. However, by this time the condition of Port Victoria Pier itself was causing concern to the newly amalgamated South Eastern & Chatham Railway. Although rebuilt following severe gale damage on 29 November 1897, the wooden supports of the pier were continually attacked by marine worms and in 1901 attempts were made to encase them in concrete. Further damage to the pier was caused on 27 May 1915 when the minesweeper *Princess Irene* blew up in the Medway with great loss of life. This led to the seaward end of the structure being declared unsafe and in 1916 it was closed, which meant all trains had to terminate at the shore end of the pier. The First World War also saw a temporary gun battery placed on the pier.

In 1922, following damage to Kingsferry Bridge (that linked the Isle of Sheppey to the mainland) by a Norwegian vessel, a temporary ferry service was operated between Port Victoria, Sheerness and Queenborough until the bridge was repaired. Nevertheless this proved to be the last great flowering of life for the pier as in 1932 it was totally closed and the railway station was relocated on land. The station buildings on the pier were demolished in 1933, and in 1941 the majority of the structure was removed by the Admiralty, for which the Southern Railway received £841 in compensation. The lonely Port Victoria station finally closed on 10 June 1951 when the area was acquired for a large oil refinery and replaced by a new station at Grain. However, passenger services on the branch were withdrawn from on 2 December 1961, but the line today remains open for freight.

Hidden away in the oil refinery complex, remains of the ill-fated pier's wooden piles are still visible at low tide.

The SE&CR pier housing Port Victoria station, c.1910. The station staff poses with a 'Q' class locomotive waiting for passengers to arrive from the Sheerness ferry. *Marlinova Collection*

A train waits on Port Victoria Pier in the 1920s during Southern Railway days. The heavy wooden support piles of the pier can clearly be seen. Unfortunately, they were to prove a tasty morsel for marine worms. *H C. Casserley*

In 1932 the pier at Port Victoria was declared unsafe and closed, leaving the railway to terminate at the shore end. The station buildings were demolished in the following year. *H.A. Vallance*

The sad final remains of Port Victoria Pier. Now surrounded by industry, some of the wooden piles of the pier can still be seen at low tide. *Lens of Sutton*

GRAIN COCKLESHELL BEACH

A wooden pier used for landing goods for the village, but it was also popular with locals as a promenade. The area is now covered with industry.

UPNOR

Situated at Lower Upnor, the pier was built around 1860 by the Pier Hotel to enable paddle steamers to call. The beach around the pier was used by people from the Medway Towns, who sometimes arrived at the pier on boats from Strood and Chatham Sun piers. Other attractions Upnor had to offer included the Woodlands Park Tea Gardens (proprietor J.T. Hosgood) with its miniature railway and boating lake, as well as a café with a dance floor.

In 1928 the pier passed to the Medway Conservancy Board, who added a timber causeway in 1933. However, the pier was later demolished by a vessel.

STROOD

The first pier in Strood was erected in 1860 by the South Eastern Railway and was sited by the original railway station of the Gravesend & Rochester Railway; a few wooden stumps of this structure may still be seen today. The station was re-sited when the line was extended to Maidstone and a new pier was built closer to it by the South Eastern & Chatham Railway in 1905 at a cost of £1,520. The pier was a regular port of call for steamers of the New Medway Steam Packet Company (later the General Steam Navigation Company) and is used today by the *Kingswear Castle* and *Waverley* for excursions. The structure has been rebuilt in recent years, and in November 2005 work began on essential repairs to the brow.

A postcard of Cockleshell Beach at Grain in the 1920s featuring the wooden pier. During the summer the beach was a popular spot for locals. *Marlinova Collection*

A closer view of the Cockleshell Pier at Grain, showing the small crane on the pier head. Although used for landing goods, the pier was also a popular promenade. *Marlinova Collection*

Lower Upnor seen from the wooden pier on a snowy day on 26 March 1911, captured by a local photographer on this evocative postcard. *Marlinova Collection*

A postcard issued by Thornton Bros of New Brompton (now Gillingham) showing a paddle steamer leaving Upnor Pier. The card was posted on 18 September 1911. *Marlinova Collection*

The old iron pier at Strood looking towards Rochester. This postcard was published by the Eastgate Series, Rochester, and was posted on 19 July 1912. *Marlinova Collection*

The rebuilt Strood Pier and landing stage, photographed at low tide on 4 May 1995. *Marlinova Collection*

ROCHESTER ESPLANADE

A little iron pier situated just below Rochester Bridge, which was principally used as a landing stage for local boat owners. The pier was subsequently used as an approach to a moored restaurant ship and in 1998 was extensively rebuilt and extended. The pier is open to the public (except the extension) and has seating.

ROCHESTER BLUE BOAR

The now demolished Blue Boar Pier was an iron structure principally used by the crewman of the pulp vessels moored in the River Medway.

ROCHESTER SHIP

The Ship Pier was used by the pulp vessels, but is now used as a port of call by the *Kingswear Castle* on its journey to and from Southend.

CHATHAM SUN

In 1775 the Sun Quay and Wharf were documented as being owned by the local brewers, the Best family. However, on 3 September 1864 the Chatham Local Board of Health purchased the small jetty from the Trust of James Best and upgraded it to a pier by driving in new piles and laying a timber deck with an asphalt coating.

In 1885 the pier was rebuilt in iron by A.T.W. Walmsley of Westminster to a design by Law & Chadderton. Whilst the work was taking place, a temporary iron gangway collapsed on 26 October 1885, fortunately without injuring anyone. The pier was further upgraded in 1902 when a waiting room was added, and two years later a 65ft extension was also added. Steamers used the pier; in later years principally those owned by the New Medway Steam Packet Company.

However, in 1959 the landing stage was closed except to small boats and yachts, and in December 1972 the pier itself was closed following a fire. Fortunately, ten years later, a major refurbishment scheme was commenced by contractors John Howard & Co., and in June 1986 BBC Radio Kent moved to a new purpose-built studio by the pier. They moved to Tunbridge Wells in 2001.

In 1987 a floating pontoon landing stage was added to the pier. This remains very popular today with fishermen.

CHATHAM THUNDERBOLT

Situated inside Chatham Historic Dockyard, the pier was named after the vessel that was used as a floating pier head from 1873 to 1948. The *Thunderbolt* was built along with the *Erebus* and *Terror* at Thames Ironworks in 1856 for service in the Crimean War. They were the first iron-built warships constructed for the Royal Navy. However, they were never tested in service, as the war finished before they were completed.

The pier remains to serve the Historic Dockyard and acts as a base for the paddle steamer *Kingswear Castle*.

The attractive little iron pier at Rochester Esplanade, photographed in 1933 by Valentines of Dundee. *Marlinova Collection*

Rochester Esplanade Pier in March 2006 looking towards the Norman castle. *Marlinova Collection*

The remains of the now demolished Blue Boar Pier in Rochester seen in the 1970s. *Marlinova Collection*

Rochester Ship Pier in November 2005. The pier has been rebuilt in a similar style to Strood Pier.
Marlinova Collection

A photograph showing the pier head of Chatham Sun Pier, taken in the 1950s.
Marlinova Collection

Chatham Sun Pier in November 2005, with the pier head waiting room now all but a memory.
Marlinova Collection

Chatham Thunderbolt Pier photographed in March 2006 – mooring place of the river-going paddle steamer *Kingswear Castle*. *Marlinova Collection*

The floating pontoon of Gillingham Pier pictured in 1907 by Photocrom of London. *Marlinova Collection*

Gillingham Pier in April 2006, with the new landing stage in the foreground. *Marlinova Collection*

GILLINGHAM

The first Gillingham Pier was known as Bridge Wharf and Collier Dock and was incorporated into an extension of Chatham Dockyard. A new pier was opened on 13 February 1873 at a cost of £30,000. This was extended with an iron structure known as the Admiralty Pier because it was used by the 'trot trot' boats that maintained communication with the Royal Navy vessels anchored offshore.

In 1881 the pier was damaged by an army boat during a gale, and the Board of Health requested that the Government should pay for repairs. The army refused however, claiming the collision was caused by an 'Act of God'. In retaliation, some of the Board members proposed scrapping all lighting on the pier, which had been installed to help soldiers board the ships. Nevertheless, the lights remained after the motion was narrowly defeated.

In recent years the area around the pier has been extensively redeveloped in association with the redevelopment of the former naval base. This includes a new landing stage and entrance gate provided by Solent Marine.

A view looking towards Queenborough Pier on a quiet day after the First World War. The heyday of the pier finished with the removal of the Flushing ferry in 1914. *Marlinova Collection*

Queenborough Pier in the early years of the twentieth century showing the railway station buildings on the right. *Marlinova Collection*

QUEENBOROUGH

The pier was opened on 15 May 1876 by the London, Chatham & Dover Railway for a ferry service to Flushing (now Vlissingen) in Holland, provided by the Zeeland Steamship Company. The boat trains ran to the end of the pier after traversing a small branch off the Sittingbourne-Sheerness line.

On 18 May 1882, the pier was badly damaged by fire; services being transferred to Dover whilst rebuilding took place. A further fire occurred on 19 July 1900; the service this time being temporarily transferred to Port Victoria.

The introduction of the Harwich-Hook of Holland service in 1909 led the Zeeland Company to present larger twin screw ships on the Queenborough route. However, they had difficulty navigating the narrow Medway sandbanks and the night service was transferred to Folkestone on 1 May 1911. The day service, using smaller vessels, continued to use Queenborough Pier until November 1914.

Unfortunately the Flushing ferries never returned at the war's end and the pier saw only occasional use thereafter as a cargo berth; by 1933 it lay virtually unused. During the Second World War, the pier was used as a base for minesweepers, but the railway track was lifted in 1955 and the demolition of the pier followed. During low water, stumps of the pier's supports can still be seen.

4

SHEERNESS PIER

Although a substantial iron structure, Sheerness is a difficult pier to classify. The pier's charging of a promenading toll qualifies it as a pleasure pier, yet it was situated away from the resort area and beach of the town and had few concessions for entertainment, being principally a landing pier throughout its lifetime.

Sheerness Pier was opened on Tuesday 8 September 1835 by the Hon. Sir Charles Elphinstone Fleeming, Commander-in-Chief of the Nore for the Sheerness Pier Commissioners. Situated in the Dockyard area of the town, the wooden structure cost £4,400 to build and became the Isle of Sheppey's principle link to the mainland. Day return excursion prices from the pier during its first year were to Southend 2s, Herne Bay 2s 6d, Medway Towns 1s 6d, Margate 3s, Ramsgate 3s 6d, Clacton 4s 6d, Walton 5s and Felixstowe 6s. The pier was also used to unload goods, and for some years the Royal Mail for the Isle of Sheppey came and went via the pier.

A wooden shelter was subsequently added to the pier, used as a waiting room, toilets and booking office for the steamers. However, the number of ships calling at the pier began to decline after the London, Chatham & Dover Railway arrived at the town in 1860, bridging the River Swale for the first time in the process. In 1875 the pier was the temporary terminal for the Zeeland Steamship Company's service to Flushing before it was transferred to Queenborough Pier the following year.

The year 1884 saw the tolls for the pier put up for auction, and although the South Eastern Railway put in the highest bid, it was rejected. Had they gained control, a through service from London, via a steamer connection from Port Victoria, could have been provided. At forty-two miles, this would have been ten miles less than the LCDR route.

In the early 1890s, a colourful local character, Edward Greenstreet, became Pier Master. He had previously run three different public houses on the Island. Unfortunately, on 29 November 1897 the pier suffered severe damage during a great storm; as described by an eye witness:

> The pier looked like a huge sea serpent, the deck following the contours of the waves as it floated on the water simulating the body, whilst the 'pavilion' appeared to be its head. As the deck (of the pier) rose and fell, it drew the piles from the sea bed.

Fortunately, Sheerness Council arranged for the pier to be rebuilt with iron piles and it was re-opened in 1899. The new structure included a baggage line with a passing loop and a shelter on the pier head that doubled as a tea room. A 1d charge was made for promenaders and a band sometimes performed on the pier head. Paddle steamers occasionally called, bound for Southend, Rochester, Chatham, Clacton, Margate, Strood, Port Victoria, Greenwich and London.

During the Second World War, the pier was requisitioned by the Royal Navy and was used to land troops during the Dunkirk evacuation. In 1946 a tug smashed through the structure, and although the Admiralty repaired the damage, they closed the pier in 1955 on the grounds it was unsafe. A scheme by Sheerness UDC to repair it sadly came to nothing because of the high cost.

The pier was sold to William Hurst Ltd, who used it to moor vessels, and then in 1965 to the Medway Ports Authority, who demolished it in 1971 to facilitate construction works in the docks.

The original wooden Sheerness Pier destroyed by a storm on 29 November 1897. This postcard was published by John A. Doughty of 13 High Street and was posted on 23 October 1906. *Marlinova Collection*

The tollhouse of Sheerness Pier, photographed in 1891. The Pier Master Edward Greenstreet is shown, along with his wife Mary, son Thomas and daughter Alice. *Sheerness Library*

The second Sheerness Pier under construction in 1898. Its wooden predecessor had been wrecked by a storm the previous year. *Sheerness Library*

An unusual view of Sheerness Pier taken by Hall Series and posted on 24 March 1908. Taken from the pier head, it shows the stairs that led up to the upper deck of the waiting room. *Marlinova Collection*

Another view of Sheerness Pier Head, with a passing Royal Navy vessel attracting the attention of those relaxing on the pier. *Marlinova Collection*

Sheerness Pier looking towards the pier head, *c.*1910. The left-hand side of the deck shows the rails for a luggage trolley. *Marlinova Collection*

In addition to its piled pier, Sheerness also had this jetty of a more solid construction, erected in the 1920s. *Marlinova Collection*

The Cheyney Rock Pier at Sheerness was erected in 1878 to receive coal barges. The coal was unloaded by crane onto iron tipping trucks that travelled about twenty yards to a large coal storage depot. In the Second World War, the pier was breached as a defence measure and was later demolished. This postcard was issued by D.T. Whalebone 'Postcard King', Sheerness, and was posted on 31 December 1908. *Marlinova Collection*

5

TANKERTON PIER

Tankerton is Whitstable's seaside suburb and has a fine greensward slope offering a splendid panorama of the sea. The area is particularly noted for 'The Street' – a bank of shingle stretching into the sea for ¾ mile. At low tide it is a pleasurable walk and children enjoy collecting shellfish at its edge. However, for a short time, Tankerton also boasted its own man-made promenade over the sea – a miniscule pier known affectionately as the 'Iron Bedstead'.

The development of Tankerton sprang from the sale in 1890 of the Tankerton Estate for £16,000 to a group of London barristers led by Charles Newton Robinson. They formed the Tankerton Estate Company, which was incorporated on 2 July 1890 with a capital of £25,000. The company acquired the land north and east of the railway for £23,000 and announced plans for the complete development of this magnificent property as a new seaside watering place of the first class; to be laid out by A.A. Kemp.

Typical plots of 20ft x 150ft were laid out, costing £5-50 with a first payment of 10s and the balance paid in nine quarterly payments. Prospective buyers were lured to view the plots by free travel on a special train from London and a free luncheon accompanied by the Town Band. In May 1891, Mr Bannon of the 'Bear & Key' provided 300 luncheons for prospective buyers at one of the sales, but 600 people turned up and the food ran out!

Unfortunately, the buyers were not so keen to actually purchase anything, and development remained slow. The recession in the building trade was said to be partially to blame, and it was not until 1895 that four double-fronted houses known as Cliff Terrace were completed. These were later converted into the Marine Hotel. A few detached residences were erected in 1896 and roads, such as Pier Avenue, were laid out.

Pier Avenue was so named in honour of Tankerton's own little pier. This had been erected in 1894 by Homan & Rogers for £660 and was officially opened on 2 August of that year. Measuring just 112ft x 15ft, it was affectionately known as the 'Iron Bedstead' or the 'Flying Bedstead'. The pier had no tollhouses and was presumably free to use by everyone.

However, the expansion of Tankerton remained sluggish. The 150-seat, purpose-built sale room was converted into the Pavilion Restaurant by the well-known caterer Mr Offredi, and land at the east end of the estate was sold to the brewers Mackeson, who erected the Tankerton Hotel in 1902. However, a proposed pleasure pier and landing quays in 1903 never got off the drawing board. Whitstable Town Council took responsibility for the cliffs and beach frontage and laid out seats, shelters and a bandstand on the greensward. This seemed to spur further development. Cliff Terrace was utilised as a convalescent home for a London hospital and a home for orphan boys. In the First World War it was used as a military hospital.

Sadly, the Iron Bedstead never quite made it to the war years. After falling into disuse and becoming steadily derelict, it was dismantled by George Warner in 1913.

The tiny pier at Tankerton, affectionately known as the 'Iron Bedstead'. Erected in 1894, the pier was demolished in 1913. *Marlinova Collection*

A rare postcard issued by Filmer Series showing the steps that led down to Tankerton Pier from Marine Parade. *Marlinova Collection*

6

HAMPTON-ON-SEA OYSTER PIER

Now a suburb of Herne Bay, the origins of Hampton-on-Sea lay in the ambitions of the Herne Bay, Hampton & Reculver Oyster Fishery Company to develop an oyster industry in the area to rival nearby Whitstable. The company was formed in 1864 and was incorporated by an Act of Parliament on 25 July 1864 with a capital of £100,000 in £10 shares. In the following year work began on erecting a 1,050ft-long wooden pier which was to be used by the fishing boats of the company and also trading vessels from Europe (the shore section of the pier was to be rebuilt in concrete). A tramway was laid from the pier to connect it with the London, Chatham & Dover Railway. In the autumn of 1866, the pier was officially opened by the Lord Mayor of London. As part of the development, a series of freshwater ponds were dug that were fed by a brook. In addition, a public house (the Hampton Inn) and a terrace of houses were provided for employees.

Unfortunately, the company soon found itself in financial difficulty as its oyster trade declined throughout the 1870s. For a time, a London hotelier named Major Davis acquired an interest in the company with the object of supplying oysters to a chain of hotels, but this venture also proved to be a failure. By an indenture, dated 6 August 1879, the company assigned much of its property to Thomas Kyffin Freeman for building development. Freeman then announced grand plans to create the new seaside resort of Hampton-on-Sea. The pier, however, remained with the company until it was offered for sale by auction, along with the tramway and other remaining assets, on behalf of the mortgagees, on 20 July 1881.

A further terrace of houses was erected, and the christened terraces Hernecliff Gardens and Eddington Gardens were offered for auction in 1888. However, by this time, the positioning of the pier and its solid landward section was causing the westward drift of beach material to accumulate on its eastern side. The western side, where the houses were situated, was therefore not replenished and was left at the mercy of the sea. The houses were badly flooded during the great storm of 29 November 1897, and in July 1899 the house nearest the sea was undermined during another gale. By 1910 it had been taken by the waves. The remainder of the houses had disappeared by the 1920s. The damage caused by coastal erosion was memorably captured on a series of postcards sold by the eccentric Edmund Reid, who resided in one of the doomed houses. Reid was a former Detective Inspector with the Metropolitan Police and had worked on the notorious 'Jack the Ripper' murders.

The pier, meanwhile, became steadily more derelict and by the early years of the twentieth century the outer section had largely gone. Nevertheless, a plan to demolish the pier in 1898-99, in a bid to halt the coastal erosion and save the threatened houses, never took place. The derelict wooden stumps in the sea proved to be a danger to shipping, leading to large notices being put up in the vicinity with the words, 'The public are warned of the existence of a number of timber stumps or piles westward of this pier, which constitutes a danger to persons boating in this vicinity'. The coastguard also marked the site with buoys.

The concrete shore section of the pier can still be seen, along with the Hampton Inn, as a reminder of an ill-fated venture.

A stormy day at Hampton Oyster Pier, *c.* 1910. The wooden section on the right of the photograph was soon to succumb to the waves. *Marlinova Collection*

The Hampton Inn and Pier on a postcard published by Lowe & Co. of Herne Bay around 1914. The wooden section of the pier has gone, although its rocky foundations can still be seen (as they can in 2007). *Marlinova Collection*

Above left: Hampton Pier seen from the beach in May 2005, with a solitary fisherman for company. *Marlinova Collection*

Above right: A recent view from the end of Hampton Pier looking towards Hampton Inn. *Marlinova Collection*

7

HERNE BAY PIERS

Although a bathing machine was known to have been in place by 1770, it was not until 1830 that a particular effort was made to bring Herne Bay into the forefront of watering places. A grand new town was projected, laid out with streets and squares. A consortium led by civil engineer George Burge proposed a pier to catch some of the steamer trade from London to the Thanet resorts.

The Herne Bay Pier Company was formed and invited Thomas Telford to design the pier. However, Telford gave the work to his assistant Thomas Rhodes who proposed a 3,633ft wooden pier terminating in a 75ft square pier head to reach deep water. An Act of Parliament was passed on 30 March 1831 for 'making and maintaining a pier or jetty', and on 4 July 1831 the first pile of the pier was driven in. A suggested addition to the scheme, outside the powers laid down by the Act, was for the erection of a colossal hollow statue of King William IV in an admiral's uniform, to be paid for by public subscription. However, the funds for such were never collected, and a proposed lighthouse on the pier head also never materialised. Nevertheless, a 50ft-wide parade along the side was built, and stone balustrading at the pier entrance was obtained from the demolition of the old London Bridge[1].

In September 1831, one of the men building the pier was shot by a coastguard whilst involved in smuggling on the beach near the construction works. The coastguard pleaded self-defence at his trial, yet the plea failed and he was sentenced to two years' hard labour for manslaughter.

During the pier's construction, Rhodes was diverted by Telford to a more prestigious job in Ireland, and George Abernethy was left in charge of the project. On 12 May 1832, the *Venus* became the first steamboat to arrive at the pier, but the works were not fully completed until September at a total coat of £50,000. The Herne Bay Pier men celebrated the completion of the pier by playing a game of cricket against the Herne Street Club, which they lost by 51 runs.

Venus was joined on the London run by the *Royal Sovereign*, and to ease the course of passengers, the lengthy pier rails were laid along the western side of the structure. On 13 June 1833 the pier's first transport, a wind or manually propelled vehicle dubbed *Old Neptune's Car*, made its first run. In that same year, Lieutenant Busbridge of the coastguard seized twenty-six kegs of contraband lying under the supports of the pier.

In 1834 the Herne Bay Steam Packet Company (also known as the London, Herne Bay, Canterbury and Dover Steam Packet Company) was formed and ran services from the pier using the 400-ton steamers *City of Canterbury*, *Red Rover* and from 1838, the *City of Boulogne*. Many people used the service to make their way to Canterbury and Dover by coach after landing at the pier. One such person was the Duke of Cambridge, on 20 September 1837, who was saluted by a battery guns on the pier head[2]. The duke took refreshment at the Pier Hotel, which thereafter became the Royal Pier Hotel.

The new steamer service appears to have initially been a success. In 1835 Thomas Henry Sinnot, clerk to the Herne Bay Pier Company, reported to the House of Commons Select Committee that 30,402 persons had embarked from the pier. This was almost twice the number that had alighted in the previous year.

A rather fanciful view of the first pier at Herne Bay dated 4 May 1832. The statue of William IV at the pier head was never in fact built. *Marlinova Collection*

The sail-driven car, dubbed *Old Neptune's Car*, that ran on the first Herne Bay Pier, 1833-62. *Marlinova Collection*

The first Herne Bay Pier pictured after closure in 1862, having been declared unsafe. The pier was demolished in 1871 to make way for a new iron pier. *Herne Bay Records Society*

Herne Bay's second pier; a small 415ft iron structure that was opened in 1873. *Herne Bay Records Society*

A £10 share certificate issued by the Herne Bay Promenade Pier Company on 10 December 1881. The company was beset by financial difficulties and the pier was sold in 1884. *Marlinova Collection*

In 1884 a pavilion was added across the entrance to Herne Bay's second pier. This view shows the pier in August 1891 when a temporary landing stage was erected to enable steamers to call. *Marlinova Collection*

Herne Bay's third pier, pictured on this postcard by Stengel, c.1902. The pavilion at the entrance to the second pier was retained, and featured a café and shops.
Marlinova Collection

However, on 28 April 1839 the pier was declared unsafe after an inspection found that many of the piles were less than half their normal thickness, and some had been severed altogether. Domestic grade wood had been used for the piles and this was being consumed, with relish, by marine borer worms. It was decided to place forty-two crutch piles under the weakest sections, until more extensive remedial work was carried out two years later. The pier remained in use whilst the work was carried out.

The pier suffered further misfortune the following year when the *Old Neptune's Car* knocked down Mrs Jane Harris, a lady with a wooden leg. Mrs Harris had been on her way to court to give evidence against a workman named Israel Jones who had been arrested on suspicion of a felony. However, he was later discharged when the lady died before she could give evidence to the prosecution.

The year 1842 proved to be a better one for the pier when record arrivals by steamboat were reported. The Herne Bay Steam Packet Company brought 40,957 passengers, whilst 11,248 more were recorded by other boats. Over 26,000 visitors were reported to have stayed in the town.

In 1844 the Pier Master, Donald Oliver Matheson, who had taken the post in 1834 and was paid £100 a year, was succeeded by Captain Cornelius Gardiner from Bristol. A local guide favoured him as a man 'whose urbanity of manner and sedulous attention to the various duties of his important office are invariably appreciated by visitors and inhabitants'. One of Gardiner's first duties was to deal with a serious accident on the pier involving a porter named George Norris, who was employed to carry passengers' luggage and push *Old Neptune's Car* along the pier against the wind. One day in July, the car was travelling at approximately 15mph when Norris jumped off to release the sail. Unfortunately the car ran over his arm, resulting in it having to be amputated at the Kent & Canterbury Hospital. Matheson was to remain Pier Master until the pier's closure in 1862.

Nevertheless, by 1847 the arrival of the South Eastern Railway to Canterbury the previous year was beginning to affect the steam packet trade to Herne Bay Pier. In evidence given to the House of Commons Select Committee, Mr S.F. Miller, Clerk to the Herne Bay Pier Company, revealed, 'In consequence of the traffic being so much decimated since the railway opened, the steamboats do not supply the place well, they do not think it worth their while, we have great difficulty in getting boats to call there at all.'

A further blow occurred in 1850 when a coach service started linking Herne Bay with Sturry station. The 1850s saw patronage of the pier decline as its condition worsened. A further accident to a member of staff occurred during the Crimean War when a salute fired from a cannon on the pier head, in honour of the siege of Sebastopol, blew porter James Stoneham's arm off.

In 1862 the pier, following a visit of the last steamer in October, was declared unsafe and closed. Three years later a provisional order in Parliament empowered the Pier Company to dismantle the seaward end of the pier, but no action was taken. Finally, in 1871 the pier was purchased by a demolition contractor for £475 and was dismantled, but the stone balustrade survived. The enterprising contractor held an auction of the timber on the beach and made a £1,000 profit on the deal. The adjoining promenade, gardens and pier approach was purchased by the Improvement Commissioners for £350.

The old pier was demolished to make way for a replacement structure promoted by the Herne Bay Promenade Pier Company. This second pier was a very different structure from its predecessor. Designed by Messrs Wilkinson & Smith and constructed of cast-iron piles filled with concrete, the new pier measured only 415ft x 21ft, leading to a 42ft pier head. Capital had been raised by the selling of £20 shares and direct labour used to construct the pier at a cost of £2,000. The pier officially opened on 27 August 1873 by Sir Sydney Waterlow, Lord Mayor of London, who travelled in state from the capital accompanied by two sheriffs in full uniform. They travelled from the station through the town, which was bedecked in flags and triumphal arches. A grand ball followed the opening and the day was rounded off with a public display of fireworks.

Admission to the pier was a penny, with season tickets costing 5s, and occasional entertainment was provided in the bandstand on the pier head. However, with the pier too short to receive steamers, the Pier Company hit financial difficulties and in 1884 the structure was sold to the Herne Bay Pavilion, Promenade & Pier Co., registered as a company on 13 December 1882. They immediately added a wooden pavilion across the entrance of the pier, which opened on 21 July 1884 by Mrs C. Prescott-Westcar, of Strode Park, Herne. Designed by McIntyre North and erected by Amos & Foad, of Whistable, the building was laid on a concrete foundation and included a felt roof that projected on all sides to form a covered way with seating against the walls. The concert/assembly room provided views of the sea. There were also dining and luncheon rooms and shops on the frontage. The cost of construction was around £3,000, and a ground rent of 5s was payable to the Local Board as lessees.

The Herne Bay Pier rink hockey team, finalists in the 1913 World Championship, photographed by Fred C. Palmer, of Tower Studio. *Left to right:* R. Fotheringham, Charlie Fox, Jack Dereham (Captain), William Hall and Horace Hall. *Marlinova Collection*

West & Son, of Whitstable, published this postcard in the 1920s showing a busy scene outside the entrance to the pier. The Grand Pier Pavilion featured dancing. *Marlinova Collection*

Right: A fishing competition in progress on Herne Bay Pier during the 1930s. *Marlinova Collection*

Opposite: The newly built Grand Pavilion on Herne Bay Pier, erected in 1910, is captured by local photographer Fred Palmer. This postcard was posted on 18 August 1911. *Marlinova Collection*

Opposite: Local photographer Scrivens captures lady diver Gladys Powsey entertaining promenaders on Herne Bay Pier. *Marlinova Collection*

Left: The Herne Bay Pier Tram, photographed by Hargreaves in the 1920s. *Marlinova Collection*

The company also aimed to increase the length of the pier to enable steamers to call again. To help achieve this aim, local solicitor and city high-flyer Henry Jones was appointed as secretary to the company. In 1890, he re-styled it the Herne Bay Pier Company and increased the capital by £25,000 with an issue of 4,300 £5 shares in order to extend the pier. A Provisional Order for the extension was granted by the Board of Trade in March 1891. Five months later, a temporary landing stage was erected to enable the paddle steamers *Empress Frederick* and *Glen Rosa* to call at high tide in order to convince locals of the steamers' desirability to call again.

By 1896, with Henry Jones now Managing Director, enough funds had been raised to start work on extending the pier. Ewing Matheson was appointed as engineer to the company, and noted pier builders Head Wrightson, of Thornaby Works, Stockton-on-Tees, were engaged as contractors. The first pile of the extension was placed by C.W. Prescott-Westcar, of Strode Park, on 26 August 1896. Two guns, which were washed overboard from the original pier in 1862-63, were recovered during the construction work and were placed at the entrance to the pier before being moved to the clock tower.

The first section of the pier was opened for business on Easter 1899, and on 14 September Mrs Prescott-Westcar performed the opening ceremony. At 3,787ft, the pier was the third longest in the country (after Southend and Southport). A tramway used during the construction was utilised to carry passengers to the steamers for one penny. The tram car was powered through a third rail, which consisted of a groove in the deck with a conduit below. The power, supplied by a gas engine and generator situated in the pavilion, was taken up into the vehicle by projecting arm situated underneath. The pier head was 76ft square and sported a wooden octagonal refreshment room with an upper balcony and dome, erected by Messrs Perry & Co., and a landing stage constructed of pitch pine that was available during all conditions of the tide. The 1884 pavilion at the pier entrance was retained, and in 1905 the occupants of the shops included fruiterer Frederick Tarling, tobacconist A.J. Sutton, chemists Collen & Drayton, and watchmaker and optician E. Ellwood. Giovanni Mazzoleni ran the restaurant (later acquired by P. Savoini) and the offices of the Herne Bay Pier Company were also situated in the building.

In addition to the restaurant and café, angling proved to be a popular attraction on the pier, and in 1903 the Herne Bay Angling Association was formed. At the end of the pier, divers entertained customers. These included Professor Augustus Davenport and Professor Powsey and, later, his daughter Gladys. She eventually retired to the area and lived at Broomfield.

A dramatic postcard by Scrivens of the Checkley Studio on High Street showing fire destruction of the entrance building of Herne Bay Pier on 9 September 1928. *Marlinova Collection*

Scrivens also captured the scene the morning after the fire, showing the sad remains of the destroyed building. This postcard was sent on 23 September 1928 with the sender pointing out that 'this is a photo of the fire we had on the pier'. *Marlinova Collection*

For a few years following the 1928 fire, the entrance to Herne Bay Pier was left open with no buildings. This postcard was issued by Donlion, *c*.1929. *Marlinova Collection*

The rather more modest replacement entrance is captured on this postcard, which was posted on 14 April 1931. The Cabaret Follies were appearing in the Grand Pavilion. *Marlinova Collection*

A photograph taken from a 1938 Herne Bay guide showing a tram waiting at the shore end station. *Marlinova Collection*

Another view from the 1938 Herne Bay guide, showing the long neck of the pier and tram track. *Marlinova Collection*

An aerial view of Herne Bay Pier by Valentines, posted on 24 July 1938, featuring a paddle steamer calling at the three-tiered pier head. *Marlinova Collection*

Herne Bay Pier set amidst a frozen pier on 23 January 1940. The Grand Pier Pavilion was still being used for skating during the winter. *Marlinova Collection*

During the Second World War, Herne Bay Pier was breached in two places as a defence measure. One of the gaps can be seen in this postcard produced by Photo Precision, just after the war. *Marlinova Collection*

Herne Bay Pier Tramway was never re-instated after the war, but for some years this miniature railway ran along the old track. *Marlinova Collection*

The electric tram was soon supplemented by two lighter vehicles, originally Bristol horse trams, adapted to travel fore and aft with the main vehicle, A smaller trolley was also attached for baggage. Unfortunately, on Tuesday 16 July 1901, the trolley jumped the rails and went over the side of the pier dragging one of the light cars and passengers with it. The consequences were described in this report from a local paper:

> Herne Bay was yesterday the scene of an exciting tram accident which resulted in the death of Mrs Pearce of 34 Appach Road, Brixton aged 74 years. Between 12 and 1 o'clock an electric car, consisting of one closed and two open carriages, went up the pier; and in front was an empty trolley being taken to the pier head for luggage. The lady and others got into the front trolley, which, when near the pier head, suddenly left the metals, and breaking down the palisade, toppled into the water, a distance of 20ft, dragging with it the front car, throwing its occupants into the sea. At the inquest last evening, it was shown that Mrs Pearce sustained brain concussion. The jury returned a verdict in accordance with the medical opinion that the pushing of a trolley in front of the cars should be discontinued.

The pier suffered a further calamity on 20 October 1905 when it was hit by the vessel *Clara*. She was owned by Mr Solley, of Whitstable, and captained by Edward Benney. The ship had sailed to Herne Bay from London with a cargo of timber and oats and anchored north-east of the pier head. However, by 11.30 p.m. strong winds forced the *Clara* to drag anchor and at 2.30 a.m. she smashed into the pier, breaking three of the support legs and twisting the main deck. While the captain stayed on board, the ship's mate managed to climb up the rigging and scramble onto the pier deck, whereupon he ran to fetch the coastguard. They were unable to help, but eventually, with the assistance of Mr C. Mount, the barge was dragged out of the pier.

By this time, the Herne Bay Pier Company was in serious financial trouble and its creditors, led principally by Head Wrightson, were instigating legal action against it. Matters had not been helped by the arrest of the Managing Director Henry Jones in February 1904 for embezzling finances of the Borough of Holborn in a bid to financially support the pier. Jones was a major player in the company, and in addition owned the pier's steamer *Cynthia*. In 1900-02, Jones was chairman of Herne Bay Urban District Council and also a town clerk of London Borough Council. Jones was sentenced to seven years' penal servitude, and the Herne Bay Pier Company went into liquidation on 15 January 1907.

Valentines captures the pier during the big winter freeze of January 1963. *Marlinova Collection*

Herne Bay Pier suffered its second big fire on 12 June 1970 when the Grand Pier Pavilion was destroyed by fire during refurbishment work. *Marlinova Collection*

The sea end of Herne Bay Pier photographed during the summer of 1975. *Marlinova Collection*

The new Pavilion on Herne Bay Pier was opened in 1976 and is pictured here by Colourmaster during the summer of 1977. The building is principally used for sporting activities. *Marlinova Collection*

The pier passed to Head Wrightson, who manned it with staff from their London office before it was acquired by Herne Bay Urban District Council for £6,000, after the sale was authorised by an Act of Parliament on 14 April 1908. The council took out a loan for £20,000 to improve the landing stage, erect a concert pavilion and widen the deck leading to the proposed pavilion. The work to the pier was carried out by the Widnes Iron Foundry to designs by Ewing Matheson. The pavilion was designed by Percy J. Waldram, of Charing Cross and Moscop, Young & Glanfield, of Bond Street, and erected by Messrs W. Pattison Ltd. The winning design had been the subject of a £2,000 competition and consisted of a timber structure on a steel frame, which was erected at the shore end of the pier where a marquee had previously existed. Erected in just seven weeks at a cost of £4,243, the pavilion consisted of a 130ft x 95ft auditorium, with refreshment rooms either side of it and an upper promenade deck. On 3 August 1910, the Grand Pier Pavilion was officially opened by Sir John Knill, Lord Mayor of London, in front of seven Kentish mayors.

The Pier Pavilion quickly became renowned, not so much for the entertainment provided, but for its internationally celebrated hockey team. This was formed on 9 December 1910, just a week after the pavilion opened for roller skating with a display of fancy and trick skating by Professor and Mrs Le-Bear. The captain of the team, Jack Derham, was one of the finest players of his day. Other regular team members included Charlie Fox (goalkeeper), William Hall, Horace Hall, Ernest Langwell and Robert Fotheringham, who played in packed houses of up to 1,600 people. The pavilion was host to the 3rd International Amateur Rink Hockey Tournament in 1913 when the pier team lost to Nelson 0-3 in the final. The same year saw them win the Kent Rink Hockey League and lose in the semi-final of the Southern Counties Cup. In the following year they were once again runners-up in the International Amateur Tournament. By 1926 the team had won the Championship of England, the Victoria Cup, three times.

The paddle steamer trade had been the principal reason why the pier had been greatly extended in the late 1890s and it remained a feature of the pier for many years. The pier's own steamer *Cynthia* had principally run to Southend and Margate, while the small vessel *Audrey* ran to Herne Bay from Rochester calling at Southend and Sheerness. The *Princess of Wales*, operated by the New Medway Steam Packet Company, covered the same route and also operated trips from Herne Bay Pier out to the Girder Light costing 1s (for children) and 6d. A regular caller at the pier was the famous *Medway Queen*, from trips to Margate, Southend, Clacton, London and the Medway towns. In 1925, the landing stage was extended with two new wings to accommodate steamer traffic.

Closed since 1968, the long neck of Herne Bay Pier finally succumbed to waves on 11 January 1978. A further section was lost a year later and the remains (except for the pier head) were removed in 1980. *Marlinova Collection*

The isolated pier head café of Herne Bay Pier seen from a boat during the 1980s. *Marlinova Collection*

Herne Bay Pier in 1999 with the pier head still isolated at sea. *Marlinova Collection*

In August 1925, a new petrol-electric tramcar, built locally by the Strode Engineering Works, was introduced. However it proved to be unreliable and was relegated in 1936 to run in tandem with a battery car.

On Saturday 9 September 1928, the old pier entrance building succumbed to a spectacular fire that burnt it to the ground. The fire was discovered at 11 p.m. as a huge crowd came to view the spectacle. The glow could be seen up to thirty miles away and the blaze was not brought under control until 3 a.m., but the remains smouldered until Monday morning. The council took the opportunity to open the entrance and make it more inviting, and erected only a modest replacement.

Fortunately, the pier enjoyed a relatively trouble-free 1930s. However, with the coming of the Second World War, two gaps were blown in the pier in 1940 as a defence measure; a 40ft breach just north of the Pier Pavilion and an 80ft one near the pier head. In the latter part of the war, the pavilion was used by the furniture manufacturer, Maples, for making camouflage netting.

After the war, the gaps in the pier were closed only with timber bridges that were said to be temporary, but in fact remained permanent. This meant that the tramway could no longer operate, and in 1950 the rolling stock was sold for scrap, but a miniature railway was operated by Mr Liversedge on the section of the pier between the gaps.

Unfortunately, the half-hearted restoration of the pier had left it in a weakened state, which was worsened by vibration from ice flows following the thaw of the big winter freeze of 1962-63. The long neck was allowed to deteriorate, and in September 1968 it was declared unsafe and closed to the public. Worse was to follow two years later when on 12 June 1970 the Pier Pavilion was destroyed by fire during refurbishment work caused by a spark from welding equipment.

A replacement pavilion, housing an aquarium, sports room, skating rink and a 100ft-high tower was prepared in February 1971 by local architect John Clauge, but the £300,000 cost was deemed too high. In 1974 the pier passed into the hands of the Canterbury City Council and a new building was prepared as a sports hall, which was opened by Sir Edward Heath on 5 September 1976.

Whilst the future of the shore end of the pier was assured, the long neck was left to the mercy of the elements. On 11 January 1978, the inevitable happened and the pier was breached into two places during a great gale that also wrecked the piers at Margate, Hunstanton and Skegness. Further sections were washed away during another storm in February 1979. The remains of the neck were removed in 1980, but the pier head, still housing its 1899 building, today remains stranded out to sea.

The surviving 335ft of the pier, principally consisting of a sports centre, but also housing a café, is well maintained and remains a feature of this re-invigorated resort. However, many in the town, including Herne Bay Association of Hotels, Business and Leisure, would like to see the pier rebuilt to extend to the isolated pier head. In 2003, a group of developers, including Marks Barfield, of London Eye fame, came together to develop ambitious proposals at an estimated cost of £4.9 million. A new pier would incorporate a monorail, sea life centre, observation tower, multi-purpose conference building and hotel, and a sea cat service which would run to and from London. The Canterbury City Council agreed to contribute £40,000 towards a feasibility study, but the scheme hit the buffers after the council indicated they could not foresee raising any part of the sum required.

Notes

1 The stone balustrade survived until it was wrecked in the Great Storm of 1953.
2 The pier's guns were also fired on 2 October 1837 to honour the official opening of the clock tower.

8

MARGATE JETTY

The first landing stage at Margate was said to have been erected around 1320 and was used to land both passengers and goods. However, the town's small harbour was left high and dry at low tide, and the transfer of passengers from the hoys and steamers to the shore usually had to be carried by local boatmen in their small craft; much to the discomfort of the passengers.

To alleviate the problem, a committee was formed by the Margate Pier & Harbour Company in October 1822 to investigate the building of a low-water landing jetty. Designed by Dr Daniel Jarvis, chairman of the Margate Pier & Harbour Company, work began in early 1824, and the 'Jarvis's Landing Stage', as it was known, was completed by April of that year. Constructed of English Oak at a cost of £8,000, the landing stage was 1,120ft in length and rose in height towards its end. However, this often led to the centre of the structure being completely covered by the sea at high tide, and it was not uncommon for promenaders to be left stranded at the end of the pier. Local boatmen went out to rescue them, but at a price!

In 1828, an ornamented cast-iron gateway was added to the entrance in honour of Dr Jarvis, but the landing stage itself suffered frequent damage from both marine worm *teredo navalis* and stormy seas. It proved to be a heavy financial burden to its owners. For example, in September 1833, 170ft of the structure was washed away during a storm. It was rebuilt using iron piling for the landing stage and seaward end. Unfortunately, another storm on 4 November 1851 breached it in two places, leaving gaps of 34 and 70ft. It was decided to demolish what remained, which was carried out in 1852–53.

Plans for a replacement landing stage were quickly implemented, which proved to be innovative for three reasons. Firstly, iron was to be used for the supporting columns rather than wood as it was far more resistant to corrosion from the sea. This was the first major structure of any length to be constructed of cast iron. Secondly, to firmly fix the piles into the seabed, screw piles were also used for the first time in a pier of this kind. Thirdly, the building of Margate's new landing stage also marked the pier-building debut of Eugenius Birch, the doyen of pier engineers who was to go on to build fourteen other structures, including Blackpool North and Brighton West.

The contractor Samuel Bastow, of Hartlepool, commenced work on the new pier after the first pile had been driven in on 3 May 1853 by George Yeates Hunter, chairman of the Court of Directors. Bastow's tender of £10,750 was the lowest by some £12,000. The new structure consisted of fourteen trestles, comprising four piles in each trestle with a fifth in the centre, braced by heavy iron bars and vertically by diagonal rods. The wooden decking was supported by wrought-iron girders. The first section was opened on 9 April 1855. However, the contractor was dismissed the following year for failing to make reasonable progress. Bastow had found great difficulty in driving the iron piles into the chalk substrata. Furthermore, he was nearly £5,000 over budget. The work was completed by direct labour supervised by Birch. The £15,200, 1,240ft structure was finally completed in July 1856; but work on the landing stage continued into 1857, utilising some of the old iron piling of the Jarvis's Landing Stage. The new structure was christened the 'jetty' to distinguish it from the adjoining harbour pier.

Margate Jetty in its original form in the 1860s before the addition of the Jetty Extension in 1875-77. *Marlinova Collection*

A view along the Margate Jetty from the original pier head, *c.*1870. *Marlinova Collection*

Margate Jetty Extension pictured on a carte-de-visite just before its completion in 1877. *Marlinova Collection*

MARGATE.

Jarvis's Landing Place in 1820.

The Jetty at present time.

1097

An interesting postcard in the Victoria Series showing the Jarvis Landing Place and its successor the Jetty. The postcard was posted on 9 August 1905. *Marlinova Collection*

A rare carte-de-visite showing the damage to Margate Jetty caused by the vessel *Charles Davenport* on 24 November 1877. *Marlinova Collection*

The torn-up decking of Margate Jetty following the Great Gale of 29 November 1897. *Marlinova Collection*

An unusual photograph showing the bridge that linked Margate Jetty to the Marine Palace. Following the storm of 29 November 1897 it lay unused until demolished around the time of the First World War. *Marlinova Collection*

A Marine Series postcard featuring the entrance to the Jetty, *c.*1910. The ornamental cast-iron arch and camera obscura can be seen. *Marlinova Collection*

A postcard view of a busy day on Margate Jetty, posted on 9 September 1904. *Marlinova Collection*

The Jetty Extension captured by the French postcard publisher L.L. and posted on 7 March 1910. *Marlinova Collection*

An L.L. view of the shore end of Margate Jetty, featuring the Hotel Metropole. The hotel hit the headlines in 1929 when Sidney Fox murdered his mother there. *Marlinova Collection*

The entrance
to the Jetty
Extension is
captured on
this view by
Photocrom,
c.1910. Note
the rails for the
hand luggage
trolley. *Marlinova
Collection*

A Photocrom
postcard of the
bandstand on the
Jetty Extension,
c.1910. *Marlinova
Collection*

A real
photographic
postcard of the
Pier Pavilion on
Margate Jetty,
c.1910. *Marlinova
Collection*

G.P. Hoare Goodman's Studios of Margate captured this view of the Jetty Extension and the visit of the Home Fleet in 1913. *Marlinova Collection*

An unusual multi-view card of Margate Jetty featuring a visiting steamer and the attractive Pier Pavilion and kiosks. The postcard was posted on 5 July 1914. *Marlinova Collection*

Right: A poster advertising a sailing from Southend to Margate aboard the popular *Royal Daffodil*. *Marlinova Collection*

Below: The first launch of the *Lord Southborough* lifeboat off Margate Jetty in 1924. *Marlinova Collection*

Margate Jetty in the 1920s with passengers hurrying to catch the approaching steamer. Note the absence of the walkway to the old Marine Palace. *Marlinova Collection*

Margate's pier-like bathing pavilion, later known as the Sundeck, extant from 1926–90. *Marlinova Collection*

A good aerial view of the Jetty Extension, Margate, produced by Valentines during the 1930s. *Marlinova Collection*

During the great tidal
surge of 31 January and 1
February 1953 Margate Jetty
was stripped of its decking,
as this dramatic photograph
shows. *Marlinova Collection*

Margate Jetty in the 1950s
pictured on a postcard by
A.H. & B.S. Paragon Series.
The entrance now has
shops and stalls. *Marlinova
Collection*

Valentines of Dundee
capture the frozen sea
around Margate Jetty in
January 1963. *Marlinova
Collection*

The new landing stage proved to be a success, but it was prone to damage by stormy seas. Part of the blame for this must be laid at the door of Birch, who built the structure too 'low', a mistake he was to repeat with some of his subsequent piers. Nevertheless, the Margate Pier & Harbour Company announced plans to extend the jetty to provide extra landing stages, a bandstand, shelters, six kiosks and seating on a new pier head. A pavilion was also envisaged, which was added in 1878. However, the original plan, drawn up by the noted engineer George Gordon Page, for an octagonal head, was changed to a hexagonal one because of costs. Work on the Jetty Extension (as it was known) commenced in June 1875 with Andrew Handyside & Co., of Derby and London, as contractors under the supervision of Ewing Matheson. The timber piling was carried out by Messrs Kirk & Randall, of Woolwich. The head had an outer diameter of 240ft and six bridges spanned the 40ft gap to the inner hexagon of 101ft. They were supported by short timber piles of greenheart topped with iron piles. The outer supports were of elm to absorb any impact from the steamers, which also bolstered three levels of iron landing stages with strength to withstand all conditions of the tide. The first section of the extension was opened in time for Easter 1877. The Lord Mayor of London carried out the Grand Opening on 1 May. In total, the construction had cost £34,457, and a 2d toll was levied for use of the extension, but the remainder of the jetty remained free to use.

Unfortunately, later that year on the night of 24 November 1877, the wrecked hull of the barque *Charles Davenport* was driven through the shore end of the pier during a severe gale. The vessel had been advertised for sale by auction and was laid up on the rocks off Newgate coastguard station when she was washed off by the tide and went through the jetty, leaving a 60ft gap and wrecking the refreshment room. Forty people were left stranded on the Jetty Extension and spent an uncomfortable night there before being rescued. The damage was estimated at £4,000 and a claim of £7,000 was made against the owners of the wrecked vessel on the grounds of their negligence in not having the wrecked removed. The case was heard before the Court of Queen's Bench in February 1879, but the claim was disallowed.

A rare photograph taken in 1975 of the commemorative board recording the building of the jetty. *Marlinova Collection*

Above: A close-up view of the Jetty Extension in 1975. *Marlinova Collection*

Opposite: A view along Margate Jetty in its final forlorn days, photographed in 1975. *Marlinova Collection*

The isolated Jetty Extension and lifeboat house following the storm of 11 January 1978. *Marlinova Collection*

The remains of Margate Jetty in March 1981. The isolated pier head was finally removed in 1998. *Marlinova Collection*

The jetty was repaired by Messrs Paramor, of Margate, using greenheart timber piles. They were also used to widen the three faces of the Jetty Extension from 12ft to 24ft, which was completed by 1879. In the meantime, the iron-framed pavilion, complete with a camera obscura in the cupola, was erected by Handysides in 1878, and two shops were added in 1880. A gas supply system was laid along the length of the jetty, but a proposed electric tramway never materialised. A small railed luggage trolley was provided, but was rarely used. Other additions to the Jetty Extension included sheltered seating (1882), two bandstands (1889), toilets (1891), steamer ticket offices (1892) and an extension of the landing stages (1893-94).

The jetty entered a period of profitability and popularity with promenaders, largely due to its intensive steamer trade, principally to London, Southend and the French coast. In 1897, the Margate Pier & Harbour Company paid over 6 per cent interest on their stock and a profit of £1,689 was made. However, on 29 November 1897 the structure's wood decking was torn up during a terrific gale that destroyed the nearby Marine Palace. The walkway leading from the jetty to the Marine Palace was closed and later dismantled in c.1914.

The decking was repaired, and in 1897-98 lifeboat slipways were added on both sides of the jetty. Further improvements were carried out in 1901-02 when the landing stages were widened and seating arrangements improved. In July 1904, an ornamental cast-iron arch was added at the entrance to the jetty, which also boasted a camera obscura acquired from the Alexandra Palace. Herr Josef Delicat & His Viennese Orchestra was a feature of the pavilion at this time. Gold's Dandy Coons was also a popular attraction. In 1914 the pavilion was enlarged with a new concert hall featuring a glass roof.

The eastern lifeboat slipway was rebuilt in 1924-25 to take the new motor lifeboat *Lord Southborough*, and four years later the western slipway was demolished. The steamer service remained well used during the inter-war period. A typical journey in 1936 saw the *Royal Eagle* leave the Tower Pier at 9.00 a.m., arriving at Margate at 1.45 p.m. The fare was 8s return, and 10s on Saturdays. Aside from the *Royal Eagle*, other popular vessels on the route included the *Royal Sovereign* and *Queen of the Channel* until the service was ended in 1966.

On 12 February 1938, the decking was once again displaced during a storm. Another section was removed in 1940 between the lifeboat house and Jetty Extension as a defence measure, after 46,722 troops from the Dunkirk rescue landed at the jetty. In 1941 the camera obscura at the entrance of the pier was destroyed during an air raid.

The structure was fully restored after the war but suffered further damage during the great tidal surge of 31 January 1953 when the decking was torn up and supporting piles damaged. These were repaired by filling them with concrete, but the structure suffered an additional blow on 6 November 1964 when the pavilion on the Jetty Extension burnt down. By the 1970s the cast ironwork of the jetty was in a poor state, and in September 1974 it was closed to the public. The final end came on 11 January 1978 when almost all of the structure, except for the lifeboat house and the Jetty Extension, was washed away during a terrific gale.

The Liverpool Salvage & Demolition Company was engaged to clear away the remains, but went bankrupt during the work. The RNLI engaged Brown & Mason to demolish the lifeboat slipway. However, during the use of explosives a large piece of metal travelled through the air, narrowly avoiding people on Fort Hill before embedding itself in the wall of the Britannia pub. The use of explosives was then banned. As a result, the Jetty Extension remained in situ before it was finally cleared away in 1998 by the Norfolk salvage firm John Martin, using divers to cut away the supports.

9

BROADSTAIRS HARBOUR PIER

The harbour pier at Broadstairs is said to date back to at least the sixteenth century. Constructed principally of stone and chalk enclosed within a timber and concrete shell, this postcard shows it around 1905 before it was widened. *Marlinova Collection*

Although not classed as a pleasure pier, and apparently never used as a steamer landing stage, Broadstairs Pier is nevertheless a popular promenade and resting place. In years gone by it was used by the famous Uncle Mack's Minstrels and in August bands played on it during the Broadstairs Folk Festival. This photograph of the pier was taken in February 2002 (for a more in-depth history of this pier read *Broadstairs Harbour* by Bob Simmonds). *Marlinova Collection*

74

10

RAMSGATE PROMENADE PIER

Initially a small fishing village in the parish of St Lawrence, Ramsgate, began to grow in importance from the fifteenth century as a limb of the Cinque Port of Sandwich. In 1578 an extension of the harbour enabled vessels of the East India Company to use the port, and Ramsgate began to flourish as Sandwich declined. From 1749 to 1791, the harbour was greatly extended, as in 1785 an Act of Parliament allowed Ramsgate to pave, light and cleanse its streets and open a public market.

By this time, Ramsgate was also finding favour as a fashionable watering place and was accumulating a fine collection of Georgian and Regency terraces, squares and crescents. The first regular steamboat service began in 1820, but they had been calling at Ramsgate since 1816. By 1827, the General Steam Navigation Company was running daily sailings from Ramsgate to Margate (to connect with the London service) and twice weekly direct sailings to the capital.

The town's impressive harbour meant there was no need for a landing pier. However, in 1878 a proposal was put forward to provide the resort with an iron promenade pier. To provide Ramsgate with a pleasure pier, the Ramsgate Promenade Pier Company was registered on 20 December 1878 with a capital of £15,000 (15,000 shares of £1 each). The company's office was originally located at 2 Granville Marina, but they later moved to Effingham House. Their prospectus heralded the fact that piers at places, such as Brighton, Blackpool, Hastings and nearby Margate, paid dividends between 7 and 12 per cent. The prospectus further claimed:

> The Company is formed for the purpose of providing a commodious promenade pier to the inhabitants of, and the numerous visitors to, Ramsgate, St. Lawrence-on-Sea and the neighbourhood. The Pier will be constructed of ornamental ironwork of the strongest form and will comprise a promenade 30ft in width, extending seaward about 500ft. At its termination seaward there will be a large and ornamental head commanding extensive sea and coast views.

The Board of Trade granted a fifty-year lease on 24 June 1879 at a peppercorn rent of 5s per year for a piece of land at the eastern end of Ramsgate Sands, where the Marina Incline Road joined Granville Marina.

However, the shares were taken up rather slowly, only enough for around 300ft of the pier to be erected. Yet it was decided to proceed with its construction in the autumn of 1879. The engineer Henry Robinson had laid plans for a simple, yet attractive, wrought-iron structure with each set of supporting legs containing three cast-iron columns and screw piles; the outer two screwed into the beach at an angle. The contractors engaged to erect the pier were pier builders of the highest pedigree: Head Wrightson, of Stockton. Based at the Teesdale Ironworks, Thornaby-on-Tees, in Stockton, Head Wrightson was one of Britain's leading engineering contractors, involved also with nine other pleasure piers.

As the work progressed, the pier company decided the pier should be completed to a length of 550ft, even though they had not the funds to pay the contractors for such a relatively short

A view of Ramsgate
Promenade Pier as
first built *c*.1882.
KCC Libraries

In February 1888
Ramsgate Pier was
leased to Thompson's
Patent Gravity
Switchback Company,
which erected
this early wooden
rollercoaster on the
deck. The ride was
in place for less than
three years before
being demolished
in January 1891.
Marlinova Collection

A rare side view
of the switchback
railway on Ramsgate
Pier showing plenty
of bathing machine
activity in the
foreground. *Marlinova
Collection*

pier. The final cost of the pier was to be nearly £12,000. Yet by 2 July 1880, only 325 shares had been taken up, including fifty each by Henry Robinson, Charles Head and Thomas Wrightson! The company's decision would soon come back to haunt them, but all that was forgotten when the pier was officially opened on 31 July 1881 to the hail of joyful noise, as 1,500 people passed through the turnstiles on the first day, each paying 2d admission (1d for children) to listen to Hawthorne's Band. However, the daily attendance figures quickly settled down to a far more moderate total, and with the revenue not being generated to pay off the debts owed to the contractor, the pier company soon found itself in financial trouble. The pier's initial attraction of just two shelters/kiosks at the seaward end was not enough to attract visitors and townsfolk to walk to the far end of the sands to frequent it. The option of landing steamer passengers at the end of the pier was also a non-starter, for Ramsgate Pier was one of the few pleasure piers that never had a landing stage. With Ramsgate already boasting a fine harbour, the pier could not compete for boat traffic; it was purely a pier for pleasure.

The fragility of the company's position was hit home at its 3rd Ordinary General Meeting at Ramsgate Town Hall on Friday 17 March 1882 when the balance sheet, up to 31 December 1881, was presented. It was reported that 63,307 persons had passed through the turnstiles since the opening day, bringing in £270 with 1s and 2d, yet the profit/loss account on the daily pier operation showed a deficit of £135 with 16s and 11d due to the cost of staff wages, hiring bands and other expenses.

Unfortunately, the situation failed to improve in 1882, and with Head Wrightson instigating legal action because they were still owed £3,840, the Ramsgate Promenade Pier Company finally imploded. On 28 April 1883 it was ordered to be wound up. Only 6,336 out of the 15,000 shares had been sold and the company owed £5,306 to its creditors. The pier was sold at auction to Head Wrightson for £2,000 and formally became their property on 16 May 1884. The Ramsgate Promenade Pier Company was officially dissolved on 5 August 1884.

In a bid to improve the fortunes of the pier, Head Wrightson added a pavilion on the pier head. Measuring 75ft x 28ft, the building held 500 people and was supported by iron pillars and girders within a wooden framework. A music and dancing licence was granted in 1885, but an application for an alcohol licence was refused, and would not be granted until 1895.

On 13 February 1888, the Promenade Pier was leased to Thompson's Patent Gravity Switchback Company Ltd for three years at an annual rent of £350 per annum, or 5 per cent of the gross takings, whichever was greater. The company began work almost straight away to erect a switchback railway along the whole of the pier deck. However, the opening of the switchback was delayed due to concern over the flimsiness of the stays securing the railway to the top of the pier's columns. Eventually, in September 1888, the ride was opened and many joyful Ramsgate children, and adults, rushed to the end of the pier and handed over their precious tuppence for the thrill of a rollercoaster ride over the sea. The experience must have been exhilarating, but in January 1891 the ride was dismantled upon the termination of the switchback company's three-year lease.

Diving demonstrations off the end of the pier was a longer-lasting attraction. Ramsgate's own Miss Lizzie Beckwith was the pier's most popular diver, as she would also carry out swimming demonstrations in a large glass tank.

Another attraction was the camera obscura run by George Scamp with its rotating periscope lens head, which reflected a panoramic view of the sea and sands onto the mirrored table in the small darkened kiosk. One particular customer who made good use of the attraction was the CID officer who spotted a well-known local crook pick-pocketing on the sands and promptly left the pier to arrest him!

The pavilion also featured military bands and dancing, as well as sacred concerts on Sundays. The Pier Pavilion was leased out each summer season. In 1891 the pier was under the direction

Ramsgate Pier entrance in 1887 featuring the attractive tollhouses, similar in style to the kiosk which still stands by the old Granville Hotel. *Marlinova Collection*

Detail of the simple pier pavilion of Ramsgate Promenade Pier. *Marlinova Collection*

Promenade Pier

RAMSGATE.

Proprietors   The RAMSGATE MARINA, PIER, & LIFT CO., Ltd.
Manager   ..   ..   Mr. F. C. DEW.

GRAND BATTLE OF

CONFETTI

SATURDAY, 10th Sept., 1898,

At 7 o'clock.

GRAND ILLUMINATIONS

MISS LIZZIE

BECKWITH,

In her Marvellous Performance in the Crystal Tank at 7.30.

DANCING!

IN THE PAVILION.

Madam HIRSCH'S Anglo-Viennese Ladies' Orchestra at 11, 3, & 7.30.

Admission to Pier   -   2d.

W. MARSHALL & SON, Printers, Ramsgate.

An advertisement for the attractions on Ramsgate Promenade Pier on Saturday 10 September 1898. *Marlinova Collection*

of H.E. Angless, and admission for adults was 2*d*, and for children under ten, 1*d*. The H.E. Angless Bijou Orchestra performed daily selections of music at 11 a.m.. There was also free variety entertainment each evening at 7.30 p.m., followed by dancing until closing. The sacred music provided each Sunday was held from 8.30 to 9.30 p.m., with free seating.

Unfortunately, each successive lessee struggled to make the pier pay and Head Wrightson was keen to get rid of it. Their prayers were answered in 1894 when they were approached by the newly formed Ramsgate Marina, Pier & Lift Company, which had been formed to purchase both the pier and the adjoining Marina Palace of Varieties. The pier was sold for £6,000. However, as the sale was taking place, the 21 March 1895 edition of the *Kent Coast Times* reported: 'On Thursday 14th, shortly after midday, the Ramsgate smack *British Queen* (skippered by Parnell) drifted and fouled the Marina Pier, carrying away the vessel's mizzen mast, post, fore rigging and damaging the bulwarks. The ironwork of the pier was extensively damaged.'

The pier was repaired, but in May 1895 it suffered another mishap when the *Kent Coast Times* on 9 May 1895 reported: 'There was a fire on the marina pier shortly after 5 p.m. on Monday evening (6th). A large portion of the decking (45 x 20ft) was destroyed while the pier was being repainted.'

The pier re-opened for the season on Monday 1 July 1895, the first under the ownership of the Ramsgate Marina, Pier & Lift Company, with F.C. Dew managing both the pier and Marina Theatre. The pier was decorated with flags and fairylights, and the day was rounded off with a grand fireworks display.

Amongst the entertainment put on by Dew on the pier were theatrical and variety shows in the pavilion, free concerts each evening at 7.30 p.m. and dancing from 9.30 to 10.30 p.m.. The Gilbert King Operetta Company was another attraction. Admission to the pier remained at 2*d*, and divers continued to be a popular feature. In August 1895 Minnie Johnson dived off the pier twice daily, and in the following month the Beckwiths (comprising two ladies and a man) gave diving and swimming displays.

The Marina Company also provided a new refreshment buffet on the north side of the pier head in the former shelter/kiosk. The south side kiosk was to be similarly converted. On 2 September 1895 the buffet was granted a wine and beer licence. A spirit licence was added on 1 September 1896.

For the 1896 season, a cinematographe was installed in the Pier Pavilion and shows were given daily at 11.45 a.m., 5 p.m. and 7 p.m. The pier and Marina gained three constables when William Wilson, Thomas Clarke and William Fogwell were sworn in.

From July 1899 the pier opened daily with admission at 2*d*. A typical day's entertainment featured Lila Clay's Ladies Orchestra at 1 a.m., Lizzie Beckwith diving from the pier and a swimming demonstration in a crystal tank at noon, Lila Clay's Ladies Orchestra at 3 p.m., the Grand Battle of Confetti and Dancing to Lila Clay's Ladies Orchestra at 7 p.m., and concluding with A Grand Display of Fireworks.

The Zingari Ladies Orchestra, with conductor Clara Muntz, were the attraction on the pier for the 1900 season. However, there was criticism in some quarters that the pier was only open between July and September. On 24 December 1901 the *Kent Coast Times* reported, 'As for that hopeless two penny pier, apparently allowed for the greater part of the year to look after itself, well when the marina is taken in hand then this neglected extension will of course be benefited.'

Both the pier and Marina benefited from the management of Fred Pollard for the 1902 season, which proved to be quite successful. Nevertheless, within three years the Ramsgate Marina, Pier & Lift Company would apply to be wound up, claiming they had been hit by competition from the newly opened Royal Victoria Pavilion. Heavily in debt, the company's share subscription was undersubscribed with only 4,868 of the shares taken up by 13 June 1904. The winding-up order was passed on 17 February 1905. However, the Ramsgate Marina, Pier & Lift Company would not be officially dissolved until 10 March 1911.

Following the demise of the Ramsgate Marina, Pier & Lift Company, the liquidator sold the pier and Marina for £600 in July 1905 to Colonel Alexander Burton Brown and Charles Ambrose Wilks, but the transaction was not officially sealed until 14 March 1906.

For the 1908 season, Dew engaged the Zingari concert party, diver Professor Davenport and fancy & ornamental swimmer Miss Ada Ward. There was also select dancing with Muntz's Orchestra and sacred concerts. However, by this time concerns were being expressed over the poor condition of the pier due to a lack of maintenance. On 20 February 1908 Ramsgate Harbour engineer Lewis Longfield reported, 'The Marina Pier is in a thoroughly dilapidated state. The decking requires renewal and guard rails require chipping and painting. But above all, the ironwork of the main structure should be thoroughly overhauled. I look upon this as absolutely necessary for the structural safety of the pier itself.'

A notice was served to Brown and Wilks to carry out repairs prior to 1 May 1909. However, by 13 April 1909, only a small portion of the decking had been renewed and the wrought ironwork above the high-water level was seen to be badly corroded. By 11 June the decking had been renewed, but the corroded ironwork lay largely untouched. The pier was subjected to another thorough examination and it was recommended the structure should be closed unless the outside girders in the first 34ft bay from the shore were strengthened by angle brackets. In addition, the weakened section of the pier was to be closed off during busy periods, such as August Bank Holiday.

Little work appears to be done, yet the pier opened for the 1909 season with the White Stars concert party and ornamental swimmers Dickenson & Johnson. The Harbour Engineer made a visit to the pier on August Bank Holiday to find it virtually deserted, and quipped that this was always the case. He noticed that a few minor repairs had been carried out, and Dew reported to him that Brown and Wilks were trying to sell the pier.

In August 1910, Harris the Sign King Company expressed interest in the pier, wishing to erect amusements and a lower platform for fishing and bathing. However, the Board of Trade refused to sanction a transaction until the pier was fully repaired. Nevertheless, proposals were drawn up in March 1911 for Harris the Sign King, in partnership with the Joy Wheel Syndicate, to sublet the pier for five years. A Joy Wheel was to be erected in the Pier Pavilion. A helter-skelter lighthouse, swings and other small amusements/sideshows would be placed upon the pier deck as well. Admission to the pier was to be free on weekdays. On Friday 5 May 1911, T.S. Mackin was granted authority to sell on the pier in place of F.C. Dew, whose long involvement with the pier came to an end.

The Joy Wheel was an amusement ride where everyone sat on a circular platform, which revolved ever faster until everyone had been spun off. On the pier deck, the small amusements and refreshment booths were indeed provided (but no photos have shown a helter-skelter), yet the pier faced stiff competition from cinemas and skating rinks, which were all the rage.

With the coming of the First World War in 1914, all amusements on the Promenade Pier were closed and the pier was left to the free reign of a few anglers. By now the pier was in a shabby condition. There was even a suggestion it should be demolished in case it was used by an invading army of Germans as a landing stage. This was never carried out, but it was an eerie premonition of what was to happen to many South and East Coast piers during the Second World War when the same sentiments led to sections of them being blown up.

A few of the anglers were on the pier during the evening of Saturday 13 July 1918 when one of them carelessly threw a lighted match onto the decking close to the pavilion. The wooden

A view along an almost
deserted Ramsgate
Promenade Pier in
c.1900. *Marlinova
Collection*

This fine view of
the Promenade Pier
at Ramsgate was
taken by the French
photographer L.L.
in c.1907. *Marlinova
Collection*

The sea crashes
against the wall
of the Ramsgate's
Granville Marina as
the Promenade Pier
looms in the distance.
Marlinova Collection

A close-up view of
Ramsgate Pier's simple,
yet attractive, ironwork.
Marlinova Collection

Ramsgate Promenade
Pier pictured just before
the outbreak of the First
World War in 1914. A Joy
Wheel has been placed
in the pavilion, and small
amusements and kiosks
line the deck. *Marlinova
Collection*

Pictured just after the First
World War, the fire and
mine damage to Ramsgate
Pier in 1918-19 can be seen
on this postcard of a very
busy beach scene. *Marlinova
Collection*

frame of the building was bone dry due to a sustained spell of hot weather, and it was soon ablaze. The anglers were sent scampering to the shore, and at 7.20 p.m. the fire brigade was summoned. Upon their arrival however, it was found that the sea end of the pier was a mass of flame, which was being fanned by a strong south-westerly wind. Moreover, the efforts of the firemen were to be hampered by additional difficulties. Water could not be drawn from the sea due to a low tide, whilst the fire engine was unable to proceed along the pier due to the profusion of stalls and amusements which had remained, despite their lack of use, throughout the war. Furthermore, the supply of water from the hydrant on the marina was totally inadequate to provide strong enough pressure through the long hose, and an additional supply had to be sought from the hydrant on the cliff near the Hotel St Cloud. All the while the blazing wood and white-hot metal of the pier were sending up huge showers of sparks to thrill the watching crowd before collapsing into the sea, causing great masses of steam to rise back over the pier.

Eventually, by 10 p.m, the blaze was finally brought under control and was almost out, but a number of firemen remained overnight to dampen the dying embers. By morning the seaward end of the pier was a blackened mass of scorched ironwork, with two large pieces of sheet iron which had formed the roof of one of the wooden buildings lying on the pier.

For a pier that never paid its way through its lifetime, the fire appeared to put to rest any hopes of re-opening following the war's end. This was to be sadly confirmed when two additional incidents caused structural damage to the supporting columns. A barge hit the pier after drifting from its moorings in Pegwell Bay. Then on 8 February 1919, a mine exploded near the pier causing some of the supports to be blown away. The mine had washed ashore on the sands by the pier and became wedged in a group of rocks. The beach was cordoned off, but at 1 p.m. the mine exploded and shook not only the pier, but the whole town. The houses on the Marina were worst hit when all their windows were blown out, and on the cliff properties also suffered damage, in particular the Hotel St Cloud.

The pier now presented itself as a very forlorn figure; its last hope of salvation dashed when Ramsgate Corporation declined to buy it in the summer of 1919. Yet the old structure was to remain a thorn in the corporation's side throughout the next decade as criticism mounted as to why they did nothing to either repair or demolish it, even though theoretically it had nothing to do with them! Among the suggestions for refurbishment was to replace the shattered head with an up-to-date bathing pool, using a re-decked pier as the walkway. However, the people of Ramsgate were clearly embarrassed by the state of the pier. Some even referred to it as the *bete noire* (pet hate) of the town's ratepayers, despite the fact they had never paid for its upkeep because it was always privately owned!

By the end of the 1920s, the old Promenade Pier was in a dilapidated state, and despite its barricaded entrance, men, and particularly boys, continued to climb on it to fish. In June 1929, a boy fell through the rotten wooden decking into the sea, fortunately without injury, and the decking was removed from the shore end of the pier to prevent a reoccurrence.

Fortunately, June 1929 also saw the pier pass into the hands of the Ministry of Transport upon the termination of the fifty-year lease. Moves were at last put in hand to demolish the old structure. The work began in June 1930, and within a short time Ramsgate's pleasure pier had been consigned to history. As a local newspaper said at the time, it was an 'un-mourned passing'.

11

PEGWELL BAY PIER

Britain's shortest-lived pleasure pier, at just five years, was conceived as part of the Ravenscliff Gardens development by the Pegwell Bay Aquarium & Hotel Company. The company was formed by James Tatnell in 1872 to reclaim 6 acres of foreshore for the gardens. Tatnell owned the Clifton Hotel in the village. The aquarium part of the scheme was later dropped, but the Clifton Hotel was enlarged, and in addition to the pier, the gardens were also to house a swimming pool, restaurant, skating rink and photographic studio.

An application was forwarded to the Board of Trade in June 1874 and work began on reclaiming the cove the following year. On 16 September 1879, the Ravenscliff Gardens and Pier were formally opened, with a basic entrance fee of 2d to use the gardens and pier, but this was increased to 6d for special occasions, such as regattas. The 300ft pier was a rather fragile structure, constructed of wood with slender iron supporting columns. A kiosk was placed on the pier head, which also had two small landing stages. However, no evidence has come to light about any vessels ever calling there, and the gardens and pier were a colossal failure, leading to the failure of the Pegwell Bay Aquarium & Hotel Company within a year of opening.

The Clifton Hotel and Ravenscliff Gardens and pier passed to the mortgage company, Sheffield & South Yorkshire Building Society, who leased them in 1880 to John Garratt Elliott, who, as a member of the London Swimming Club, was principally interested in the swimming pool. However, he departed in the following year and the mortgage company tried unsuccessfully to sell the development. It appears that in 1883–84 the gardens and pier were leased to Jane Carter at the Belle Vue Tavern (famous for its shrimp paste), but the short and rather sad life of the little pier came to an end on 4 December 1884 when the hull of the wrecked barge *Usko* drove through the shore end of the structure during a gale. In January and February 1885 the surviving portion of the pier was sold off on the cliff top.

The gardens eventually came into the hands of the Working Men's Club & Institute Union, which had utilised the former Clifton Hotel since August 1894. A corner was also used by the Conyngham Café for entertainment from 1894 to 1908. The swimming pool was filled in 1895, and the gardens over the years became unkempt. They were abandoned by the convalescent home in the late 1960s and are now overgrown. However, at low tide, the piles of the head of the long-lost pier may still be seen.

A view of Pegwell village showing the jetties that served the Belle Vue and Clifton Hotels, c.1875. They were demolished in the following year as work began on reclaiming the cove, in the foreground. *Marlinova Collection*

A rare photograph of the pier at Pegwell Bay, erected in 1879 as part of the Ravenscliff Gardens project, which included the swimming pool in the foreground. *Marlinova Collection*

The only other known photograph of Pegwell Bay Pier is this view from around 1880. In December 1884 the pier was wrecked by a ship and was demolished the following month. *Marlinova Collection*

Surviving piles of Pegwell Bay Pier, pictured in July 2001. *Marlinova Collection*

12

DEAL PIERS

The first marine structure at Deal was a wooden jetty that stretched out a small distance opposite Coppin Street. This had been erected by Mayor Josiah Lane following a visit by George II on 13 October 1740, who complained about his uncomfortable landing in town. The jetty was used by crews and passengers boarding ships at the anchor in the Downs, but was destroyed by a gale in October 1758.

The next venture was a wooden pier erected by John Rennie for the Deal Pier Company in 1838. The plans indicated a structure of 445ft in length. An Act of Parliament authorised the pier company to raise £21,000 (in 4,200 shares of £5 each) to finance the pier, which was to be situated to the north of the Royal Hotel. However, after 250ft of the pier had been constructed at a cost of £12,000, work abruptly ceased as the Deal Pier Company had run into financial difficulties. Nevertheless, the pier was opened and steamers called, but over the next twenty years the structure progressively decayed due to storm damage and attacks by sandworms[1]. By the 1850s it was described as being an eyesore, and in 1857 was completely destroyed during a storm. The wreckage was washed up on the beach and sold for £50, but the stonework at the entrance to the pier remained in situ for some time. Occasionally, at the lowest tides, some of the pier's wooden stumps can be seen today.

In spite of this unfortunate experience, there was still a great deal of support in the town for proposals to build another pier; led by the proprietor of the *Deal Telegram* Edward Hayward, who campaigned tirelessly in the newspaper for a new pier. In September 1861, the Deal & Walmer Pier Company was incorporated, and they engaged Eugenius Birch to design a new pier. Birch had already earned high regard as a competent engineer for his work on the Margate Jetty. The Scottish firm, Robert Laidlaw, was engaged as contractors, and work began in the spring of 1863 with the wife of the local MP, Mr Knatchbull-Hugessen, driving in the first pile of the pier and placing inside the column a tin box with a parchment containing details of the construction. Stone from the ruins of Sandown Castle, situated a short distance up the coast, was used for the abutment of the pier, while the pier itself was to be principally constructed of wrought and cast iron, supported on cast-iron columns screwed into the ground. The length of the structure was 1,100ft, which included a three-decked pier head and steamer landing stage. Seating ran along both sides of the pier and a tramway was provided for the conveying of goods and luggage. Two attractive tollhouses were built at the pier entrance.

On 14 July 1864, the pier was formally opened by Mrs Knatchbull-Hugessen in front of a large crowd, which included troops from the Walmer Barracks, the band of the Royal Marines and the 6th Depot Battalion. Mrs Fowler-Burton, wife of the Depot Commandant, was the first person to pay the toll to walk upon the pier. An engraving of the opening was pictured in the 19 November 1864 edition of the *Illustrated London News*, along with this description:

> There was a great concourse of spectators around the flagstaff at the pier head to witness the ceremony, which was performed by Mrs Hugessen, wife of the Borough Member, who had herself in April 1863, inaugurated the commencement of the work. The lady took her seat in

a chair which was placed on a truck and drawn along the tramway to the end of the pier. She then declared the pier opened, and congratulated the Deal & Walmer Pier Company, as well as the town of Deal upon completion of this useful structure. There was afterwards a banquet at the New Assembly Room. Mr John Attwell, Chairman of the Company, presided; and among the guests was Lord Clarence Paget, the Secretary to the Admiralty, beside the County and Borough members. Lord Clarence Paget highly commended the erection of the pier to give a readier access to the Downs roadstead and hinted that if the charges were not too exorbitant the Government might be disposed to use the Deal Pier for the embarkation of troops. It is expected that this accommodation will induce many persons to land at Deal from ships passing up the Channel.

Although very proud of its new iron pier, the Deal & Walmer Pier Company was unfortunately unable to pay for it. In 1866 they went under and the pier passed to the contactors who were owed a substantial amount of money. During the 1870s, they added a reading room at the pier entrance with admission charge of 1d, and in 1886 a pavilion was erected on the pier head. This became a popular concert party venue and was enlarged in 1897 to seat 500 people. The Unique Concert Party was a particular favourite in the pavilion. The showing of films also became popular. Band concerts were held on the pier deck, and pleasure steamers, such as the *Koh-I-Noor*, called at the landing stage. However, angling soon became the principal pastime on the pier, a position it has held ever since, and became renowned for its three-day angling festival.

Unfortunately, the pier was the scene of tragedy in 1871 when the Deal lugger *Reform* sank beneath the columns with the loss of her crew of eleven. Two years later the pier was damaged when the barque *Merle* hit it during a storm. Repairs were carried out, but on 26 January 1884 additional damage was caused by the storm-wrecked schooner *Alliance*. And on 24 March 1898 the pier head was wrecked by a gale whilst in the process of being enlarged.

Deal's wooden pier (and W. Bush's Iron Great Caisson) as sketched by Henry Moses in September 1840. *Deal Maritime & Local History Museum*

Deal Beach and the first pier captured by Henry Moses on 15 September 1840 in this pen and wash drawing. *Deal Maritime & Local History Museum*

A carte-de-visite showing the second Deal Pier in its original form, *c.*1870. *Marlinova Collection*

A rare carte-de-visite featuring the loss of the *Reform* under Deal Pier on 16 January 1871. *Marlinova Collection*

Another scarce carte-de-visite, this time showing the wreck of the *Merle* wedged under the pier on 19 January 1873. *Marlinova Collection*

Deal Pier pictured by the postcard publisher L.L., *c.*1907. The pavilion at the end of the pier was added in 1886. *Marlinova Collection*

A view along Deal Pier taken by local photographer J. Glencairn Craik and posted on 29 March 1907. *Marlinova Collection*

Deal Pier features in a delightful winter scene captured by Glencairn Craik and posted on 10 July 1907. *Marlinova Collection*

Local photographer H. Franklin captures the Home Fleet at Deal on 3 July 1908. *Marlinova Collection*

A rare postcard by J. Glencairn Craik capturing the Royal Marines Band in concert on the pier head at Deal. *Marlinova Collection*

The SS *Koh-I-Noor* was an occasional caller at Deal Pier. The steamer is seen at the pier on this postcard by E.T.W. Dennis, posted on 22 March 1911. *Marlinova Collection*

The flags are out on Deal Pier for yachting day, *c.*1911. Note the advertising on the pier's kiosks – these were later removed during the 1930s. *Marlinova Collection*

Looking towards the entrance of the pier, we view some of the attractive properties that line Deal seafront to this day. This fine postcard was issued by A. & G. Taylor's Reality Series, *c.*1910. *Marlinova Collection*

Above: This unusual postcard captures a naval picket marching along the pier on 7 July 1913. *Marlinova Collection*

Left: A programme for Deal Pier Pavilion in 1911. The Unique Concert Party was the feature, which performed both in the mornings and evenings. *Marlinova Collection*

Deal Pier has always been popular with anglers. Glencairn Craik has photographed the contestants in a ladies competition, *c.*1910. *Marlinova Collection*

There were also children's fishing competitions. Local photographer Meek has pictured Mrs Kerr's event during the summer of 1913. *Marlinova Collection*

The local fishermen are happy to pose for the photographer Glencairn Craik in 1909. *Marlinova Collection*

This aerial view of the pier gives a good view of the pier head buildings and landing stage, *c*.1935. *Marlinova Collection*

Deal Pier during the 1930s. Note how the kiosks have been tidied up from the Edwardian era. *Marlinova Collection*

The end for the second Deal Pier came on 29 January 1940 when the mine-damaged Dutch vessel *Nora* was driven through the pier during high tide. *Marlinova Collection*

The *Nora* lies on her side having gone through Deal Pier on 29 January 1940. *Marlinova Collection*

An unusual Christmas card showing the third Deal Pier under construction in 1955. Work began the previous year and would be completed in 1957. *Marlinova Collection*

1955.

Through the changing years - the Christmas Wish remains the same.

1864

The third Deal Pier pictured soon after it was opened in 1957, costing £250,000 to build. This postcard was produced by Photo Precision and was posted on 21 August 1961.

A photograph of the reconstruction work on Deal Pier in October 2003. The work involved repair of the concrete-covered steel piles and the primary beams under the pier. *Marlinova Collection*

The entrance to Deal Pier pictured in March 2005 showing the statue 'Embracing the Sea' by Jon Buck. *Marlinova Collection*

In 1920, Deal Council purchased the pier for £10,000, and during the inter-war years it continued to be well patronised, particularly by anglers. However, with the coming of the Second World War, disaster struck. On 29 January 1940, the 350-ton Dutch motor vessel *Nora*, carrying 317 tons of strawboard on a voyage from Harlingen to London, was anchored a mile offshore when she was hit by a drifting magnetic mine. A huge hole was blown in her stern, but fortunately all of the crew was rescued. The strickened vessel was towed to the beach, fifty yards south of the pier, much to the chagrin of the local fishermen who warned the authorities of what was to follow. The *Nora* remained there, partially submerged, until the rising tide lifted her from the beach and continually smashed her against the side of the pier. The gallant old structure withstood the battering for a time, but eventually the vessel was driven through the pier, causing around 200ft of the ironwork to crash down onto the wrecked ship. The pier remained in this gap-toothed condition until the visiting Winston Churchill gave the army consent to demolish it to enable their coastal guns to have a clear line of fire. All that remained was the pair of tollbooths at the pier entrance.

Strong local pressure during the post-war years was rewarded when the old tollbooths were removed in 1954 to enable work to begin on a new pier. This took three years to build and was formally opened on 19 November 1957 by the Duke of Edinburgh. Deal's third pier was the first seaside pleasure pier of any substantial length to be erected since 1910. The new structure, designed by Sir W. Halcrow & Partners and costing £250,000, was 1,026ft in length and built of re-enforced concrete. The Concrete Piling Ltd Co. erected the entire structure, which had nineteen support assemblies between the shore and pier head structure. These supports were constructed of steel piles surrounded by concrete contained in a concrete 'case'. The decking consisted of concrete slabs supported upon concrete-covered steel joists. The result was a functional, yet graceful structure, traditional in design. Modern-looking, continuous seating was provided along both sides of the pier, and on the pier head was placed a café and sun lounge. The landing stage was on three levels, but a miscalculation of the tides resulted in the lower deck being permanently covered by the sea. In common with its predecessor, the pier became renowned as one of the finest fishing venues in the south-east.

Now in the hands of the Dover District Council, fishing on the pier remains as popular as ever, and the pier head café has acquired a fine reputation for the quality of its cooked breakfasts! An eye-catching statue by Jon Buck entitled 'Embracing the Sea' was added to the pier entrance concourse. In 2001 and 2002, Deal Pier was runner-up in the National Piers Society's 'Pier of the Year' competition.

However, wear and tear on the pier structure, particularly the concrete columns, led to the council requesting Lottery funding, which was turned down. To their credit they inaugurated in 2002 the first of a three-phase restoration plan, costing between £2.5 and 2.8 million, covering structural repairs above and below water, and the building of a new café and conservatory at the pier head. Phase one would include the repair of the concrete-covered steel piles and the edge of the pier. Phase two would involve repair of the primary beams underneath the pier, and the final phase involved the tidying up of the lower decks, fishing deck and the pier head.

The tender for the work went out in the autumn of 2002 and was awarded in January 2003 to John Martin Construction Ltd, a subsidiary of Edward Nuttall Ltd since 1999, who had estimated a cost of £1.8 million for the work, which began in March 2003. A scheme was devised to keep the pier open to the public by housing the long-reach excavator and pile-breaker in a jack-up barge, which keeps the pier clear from obstruction. In order to repair the edge of the pier, an 18-ton gantry moved along the structure on skates. Because of its weight and the danger to the concrete structure, the contractors added longitudinal beams over the pier caps, thus transferring the crane's weight onto the piles rather than the concrete decking. A 16-ton limpet dam, designed to create a dry working environment below the water level adjacent to the pier, enabled work to be carried out to a depth of seven metres. The work on the piles necessitated breaking off the original cracked concrete covering, grit-blasting the exposed and sometimes corroded steel beams, then coating and re-covering them with concrete. Because of the cost, only the deteriorated piles were treated.

In January 2006, the Dover District Council announced that an Invited Design Competition was being organised on their behalf by the Royal Institute of Architects for a new-look pier head café bar, to be opened in 2007 during the Golden Jubilee of the pier. The leader of the council, Cllr Paul Watkins, declared:

These improvements will complete the £2.6m project of works for Deal Pier. The present restaurant is in need of urgent upgrading to improve facilities and to take full advantage of the potential that makes Deal Pier so attractive to visitors and local people. One of the major attractions is the tremendous view that can be seen along Deal's unique seafront. An architect's competition will give the opportunity for that view to be fully exploited, which the present café is not able to achieve. We want what is best for Deal and this is an opportunity to make the best of one of Deal's best loved settings.

Notes

1   Timber for the pier was maintained in a small alley named Wood Yard, which led off from Oak Street.

13

DOVER PROMENADE PIER

Dover developed as a minor seaside resort during the middle of the nineteenth century, despite the fact that the beach was steep and stony and had a limited bathing area. Nevertheless, whilst Dover certainly was no threat to other developing coastal resorts in Kent, it did attract an appreciable quantity of fashionable visitors each summer season, particularly from London. This led to the establishment of a few hotels (notably the massive Burlington, and the Grand), seawater baths, a reading room and the construction of an esplanade. Bathing machines were provided too, but largely due to council opposition a promenade pier for the town was a later development.

The first scheme for a promenade pier for Dover was in 1871, with the formation on the 8 February of the Dover Promenade Pier Company. A share capital of £12,000 (2,400 per £5 shares) was announced, but only seven of the shares were taken up before the company was refused an Act of Parliament to build the pier. No business was ever undertaken by the company and it was officially dissolved on 15 January 1884.

The next attempt to build a pier at Dover was more successful. The Dover Promenade Pier & Pavilion Company was formed on 27 November 1888 and was registered with the Board of Trade on 18 February 1889 with a share capital of £30,000 (6,000 per £5 shares). The first meeting was held on 17 May 1889 with Sir Richard Dickenson as chairman, and 34-36 Castle Street was set up as the registered office of the company. In 1894 it was moved to the pier entrance. Renowned engineer John James Webster won the £100 competition prize to design the pier and Alfred Thorne was engaged as contractor. The first pile was driven in on 11 December 1891, and the pier officially opened on Whit Monday 22 May 1893 by Lady Dickenson, with a cost of £24,000. Following the opening ceremony, a grand luncheon was held in the Town Hall, followed by a regatta.

Dover's new promenade pier was 900ft long and for the first 640ft the width of the deck was 30ft, after which it increased to 100ft at the pier head. The pier's cast-iron piles were firmly screwed into the chalk substratum, and were held together by diagonal and horizontal bracing. Wrought-iron girders resting on the piles supported the steel deck beams bolted to them – these carried the timber joists and deck floor boarding. The Moorish-style kiosks along the pier's length were particularly pleasing, and a pair of ornamental gates was positioned between two attractive kiosks at the entrance[1]. The landing stage was reached by an incline of cast-iron gratings on cantilevers. A pavilion was also intended for the pier head, but due to lack of funds this was not built for several years.

The pier company was very proud of its pier, but sadly disaster was soon to strike. On 11 November 1893, the Bremen-registered vessel *Christine* collided with the pier head, weakening the structure. Worse was to follow the next year when a severe storm on 14 November 1894 removed 100ft of the centre of the pier. Repairs were done by Murdock & Cameron and the pier was re-opened on 4 August 1895.

However, the pier's troubles led to financial difficulties for the already cash-strapped pier company. On 22 January 1896, a special meeting was held by the company in a bid to raise extra capital. On 15 February 1896 it was announced that the capital was to be increased by £1,000, with an issue of 200 £5 preference shares.

Dover Promenade Pier under
construction in September
1892. *Marlinova Collection*

Opened in 1893, Dover
Promenade Pier suffered an
unfortunate start when it
was rammed by a ship. The
following year a section of
the structure (seen here) was
washed away in a storm. *Dover
Museum*

A view of Dover Promenade
Pier in the 1890s taken from
a lantern slide. The pier was
similar in appearance to Bangor
Pier in North Wales (opened
in 1896 and regarded as one
of the finest surviving pleasure
piers). *Marlinova Collection*

Above: A rare view of a pleasure steamer at Dover Promenade Pier taken in the late 1890s. The bandstand on the pier head would soon be replaced by a pavilion. *Marlinova Collection*

Left: The cover of a programme highlighting the events on Dover Promenade Pier, *c.*1900. The feature was a concert by the band of the 6th Battalion Royal Fusiliers. *Marlinova Collection*

In 1901 a pavilion was added to the pier head of Dover Promenade Pier. A full view of the pier is seen here the following year. A Stengel postcard posted on 11 September 1903. *Marlinova Collection*

Another Stengel postcard, this time showing a view along the pier from the pavilion. The postcard was posted on 5 October 1905. *Marlinova Collection*

One of Dover Pier's elegant entrance kiosks is a feature of this postcard, published by Kingsway Series and posted on 9 May 1905. *Marlinova Collection*

One of the Edwardian attractions on Dover Promenade Pier was Professor Davenport diving from the pier in a sack. This postcard captures a dive on 8 May 1906. *Marlinova Collection*

Another feature on Dover Promenade Pier was roller skating in the pavilion during the winter. This unusual postcard features the skating instructor Frederick Sharp, described on the card as 'quite a lad'. *Marlinova Collection*

During the summer months, Dover Promenade Pier boasted its own orchestra, seen here in 1906. *Marlinova Collection*

A view of the Hotel Burlington taken from the Promenade Pier, *c*.1910. Sections of the entrance gates survive at Pope's Hall, Lenham, in Kent. The hotel was severely damaged during the Second World War and was demolished. *Marlinova Collection*

The body of Captain Ralph Fryatt is carried along Dover Promenade Pier in 1919. Now in the hands of the Admiralty, the pier was in use as a landing stage and known as the Naval Pier. *Marlinova Collection*

In the early 1920s the pier was leased back by the Admiralty as a pleasure pier. It is seen here on a regatta day in the early 1920s. *Marlinova Collection*

Dover Promenade Pier in the early 1920s. Notice how two of the kiosks have been moved from their original position. *Marlinova Collection*

The Promenade Pier was closed in 1926. The following year work began on its demolition. This rare photograph shows the ornate entrance gates and kiosks adorned with the demolition board of the contractor A.O. Hill, and a notice advertising the sale of building materials. *Alan Brigham*

A photograph showing the demolition of the Dover Promenade Pier Pavilion in progress. *Alan Brigham*

Two surviving wrought-iron entrance gates of the old Dover Promenade Pier still flank the entrance into Pope's Hall, near Lenham. The photograph was taken in September 2006. *Marlinova Collection*

Until it was filled with concrete during the 1960s, Dover's Prince of Wales landing pier sported attractive iron and steel work. The pier was opened on 31 May 1902 and named in honour of the Prince of Wales who had laid the foundation stone. The distinctive clock tower at the entrance remains a feature of the pier. *Marlinova Collection*

A sad episode in the pier's history occurred on 15 August 1898 when Mr A. Wells, a member of the Dover Corporation Band who was playing on the pier, suffered sunstroke and subsequently died. On a happier note, 1898 also saw the tug-come-excursion paddle steamer *Conqueror III* use the pier on service from London.

In 1899 plans were finally put in place to provide the pier with a pavilion, and a subscription list for an issue of 1,200 preference shares of £5 each was opened on 3 March. The design of J. W. Adcock was chosen and the pavilion was formally opened two years later on Monday 15 June 1901, at a cost of £6,450. The contractors, Anthony and William Fasey, received £5,450 in cash and £1,000 in company shares. A pier orchestra was formed to perform three times daily in the pavilion. Gas lighting was also provided on the pier and two small paddle steamers called at the pier on service from Margate to Folkestone. An additional attraction featured divers who jumped into the sea from the pier. These included Miss Minnie Johnson and Professor Davenport, who dived off the pier in a sack.

However, the pier was only a partial success and struggled to pay its way. In 1903 it was announced that an issue of 240 first mortgage debentures of £25 was to be raised, with an annual interest of 5 per cent and redeemable after ten years. However the scheme was not successful. By this time, some 3,959 shares had been sold by the company, including 2,639 ordinary and 1,320 preference shares.

In 1911, the pier was leased to Robert Forsyth, who had successfully transformed the fortunes of Folkestone's Victoria Pier, but in 1913 it was acquired by the Admiralty for use as a landing stage and was renamed the Naval Pier. The Dover Promenade Pier & Pavilion Company was formally wound up on 31 July 1913.

During the First World War, the pier was damaged twice by ships but remained in serviceable condition. In 1919, the bodies of martyrs Edith Cavell and Captain Ralph Fryatt landed on the pier.

In the early 1920s, the pier was leased back as a pleasure pier and was used as a vantage point during regatta days. However by 1925 the structure needed extensive repairs and the Admiralty felt that the cost was not justified. The pier was closed in 1926 and in the following year was demolished by A.O. Hill Ltd (later Dover Industries Ltd), who held two auctions in June and July 1927 to sell off the pier structure. Two of the pier gates survive to this day and grace the entrance driveway to Pope's Hall, Lenham.

Notes

1 The pier was very similar in design to Webster and Thorne's later, and much heralded pier at Bangor in North Wales which was fully restored in 1988.

14

FOLKESTONE VICTORIA PIER

The Folkestone Promenade Pier Company was incorporated on 23 February 1875 with a capital of £10,000, with the intention of providing Folkestone with a pleasure pier. In April 1877, the capital was increased to £17,500 (1,750 shares of £10 each), but due largely to opposition from the Town Council, who was worried the pier would interfere with the bathing ground, the scheme foundered.

However, by 1883 the council was far more susceptible to the idea of a pier, and in February 1884 the Folkestone Promenade Pier Company was re-incorporated by local estate agent George Bramston Trent. The company was also keen to erect a cliff lift to connect the pier to the Leas Promenade and re-named itself the Folkestone Pier & Lift Company. The Folkestone Pier & Lift Act was passed on 7 August 1884, and a capital of £40,000 was envisaged to erect an 800ft-long pier with a commodious pavilion near the shore and water-balance cliff tramway.

Unfortunately, the shares were slow to sell and the South Eastern Railway baulked at its option to take part in the scheme. A further blow occurred when the option to build the cliff lift was taken up by the Folkestone Lift Company, which opened it on 16 September 1885 with immediate success.

Undaunted, the Folkestone Pier & Lift Company announced a revised capital of £28,000, to be raised with 2,875 £10 shares, and a new design for the pier by Noel Ridley. Manchester contractors Heenan & Froude (later involved with the construction of Blackpool Tower) were engaged to construct the pier. The foundation stone was laid by Viscountess Folkestone on Saturday 7 May 1887.

The pier was opened by Lady Folkestone just over a year later on 21 July 1888. The structure boasted a fine and commodious pavilion that could seat 800 patrons. It was leased out to theatrical companies who provided suitable high-brow entertainment for Folkestone's largely aristocratic clientele. The pavilion held a six-day publican's licence and housed refreshment bars on the ground floor, as well as a kitchen, dining room, bureau and balcony on the first floor. A stroll on the pier cost 2d.

The FP&LC, however, soon found itself in financial difficulty due to the eventual high cost of the pier's £44,000 construction and prohibitive running costs. Another headache proved to be the floating landing stage erected off the pier head in 1889. This much-heralded structure hardly saw any steamer traffic and was taken out of service in 1892. Matters reached a head in 1889-90, but the company was reformed, and in 1894 the financial situation was eased following the granting of a £3,490 mortgage by the South Eastern Railway, repayable over a lengthy period at 5 per cent interest. In the same year, it was decided that the Pier Pavilion should be leased out on a permanent basis, and the large entertainment agency Keith Prowse took up the option in 1894-95. Keith Prowse was succeeded by King & Co. from 1896 to 1902. They brought the great Marie Lloyd to the pier in 1898. The FP&LC even managed to make a small profit but never enough to pay a dividend to its hard-pressed shareholders, except for the 1 per cent paid out in 1891.

In 1903, the pier company decided to lease out the whole pier to one company, and Keith Prowse returned to take up the option at the cost of £7,000 per annum, plus a percentage of the

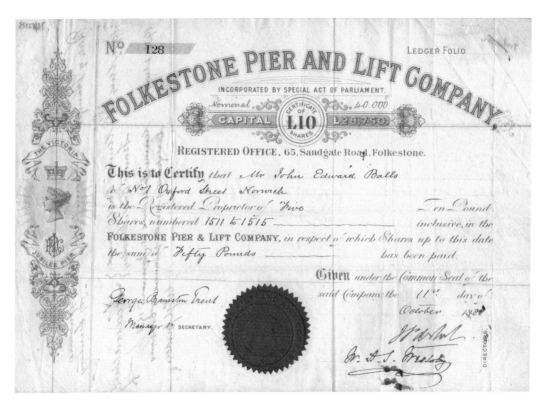

A Folkestone Pier & Lift Company share certificate dated 2 July 1888. Note how the capital has been altered from £28,750 to £40,000. *Marlinova Collection*

A view of Folkestone's Victoria Pier taken from the Leas in 1889, a year after the pier had opened. The switchback railway on the beach also opened in 1888. *Marlinova Collection*

A view of the Leas taken from the Victoria Pier in 1889 showing the Leas Lift in its original layout. An extra pair of tracks was added in 1890. *Marlinova Collection*

A close-up view of the Victoria Pier Pavilion taken from a lantern slide, *c.*1890. The floating landing stage at the end of the pier was rarely used, and was demolished around 1900. *Marlinova Collection*

Herr Moritz Würm's Viennese and Hungarian bands were a feature of the Victoria Pier Pavilion for a number of years. This programme was for a concert by the Kossuth Hungarian Band, *c.*1900. *Marlinova Collection*

A fine study of the entrance to the Victoria Pier around 1900 with an array of sweetmeat and 'What the Butler Saw' machines, as well as a fine wrought-iron sign with the date of opening. *Eddie Curry*

A postcard view of Folkestone Pier featuring the attractive cluster of kiosks at the entrance. The card was used on 6 April 1905. *Marlinova Collection*

Folkestone Pier and beach with a selection of rowing boats and deckchairs for hire, *c.*1906. *Marlinova Collection*

Above: A rare postcard by the West End Photo Co., Folkestone showing a fishing competition on the Victoria Pier in 1907. *Marlinova Collection*

Opposite: A postcard of Folkestone Victoria Pier by Harmer of Sandgate and posted on 18 August 1910. The skating rink on the right-hand side of the picture was opened that year. *Marlinova Collection*

VICTORIA PIER FOLKESTONE.

The Victoria Pier was an excellent vantage point on Folkestone's regatta days and is pictured here on this day in c.1912. *Marlinova Collection*

Folkestone's Victoria Pier seen in the 1920s. Two of the pier's main attractions are being promoted as a health benefit! *Marlinova Collection*

Right: Another attraction of the Victoria Pier in the 1920s was diver Angus Kinsela diving off the pier on a bicycle in September 1928. *Marlinova Collection*

Below: Regatta Day on the Victoria Pier in the 1920s with the Highland band leading a parade along the pier. *Marlinova Collection*

A group of ladies who participated in one of Folkestone Pier's famous beauty contests. *Marlinova Collection*

The van that drove around Folkestone advertising the attractions on the Victoria Pier. *Marlinova Collection*

In 1940 the Victoria Pier was breached as a defence precaution. Three years later the gap was bridged for a pump installation in the pavilion so seawater could be used to fight fires in the town. This photograph shows the track along the pier to transport the pump to the pavilion. *Marlinova Collection*

gate receipts. Herr Moritz Würm and his orchestras proved to be a great attraction. Some of the other big names booked to play on the pier included Dan Leno (1904), Arthur Roberts (1904), Harry Randall (1905-06) and Lillie Langtry (1906). Unfortunately, the Jersey Lily's performance in the play *Between the Night and Light* was roundly booed and she had to be escorted off the pier by police, followed by an irate crowd!

At the end of the 1906 season, Keith Prowse announced that they would not be renewing their lease. Fortunately, new lessees were soon found and proved to be a totally different kettle of fish to what existed previously. Local businessmen and councillor (William) Robert Forsyth formed the Victoria Pier Syndicate and took the lease for the 1907 season. Forsyth's syndicate was registered on 4 April 1907 with a capital of £1,000 (1,000 £1 shares), which were all taken up. Out went the formal entertainment and in came new attractions, such as novelty acts, wrestling, moving pictures and beauty contests, which were amongst the first of their kind in the world. Folkestone's well-heeled visitors turned up their noses and shunned the pier, yet it became instantly popular with the ever-increasing number of working- and middle-class visitors coming to Folkestone.

In 1909 Robert's brother, Garnet, known by his middle name of Lloyd, joined the syndicate. In the following year, Forsyth added an attraction to the pier when, at the height of the roller skating craze, the Victoria Pier Olympia skating rink was opened on the western side of the pier gardens.

Robert Forsyth was a forceful, but nonetheless popular personality who frequently flouted the law by showing the films on Sundays. He was continually fined for doing so, but as film profits

The sad state of the Victoria Pier at the war's end following the destruction of the Pier Pavilion by fire on Whit Sunday 1945. The remains of the pier were finally demolished in 1954. *Marlinova Collection*

were higher than the fines, he kept showing them! Two other attractions added just before the outbreak of war in 1914 were an open-air dancing arena on the pier deck and a rifle range.

During the First World War, the pier was popular with many troops recuperating in Folkestone's rest camps. A variety of comedy and propaganda films were shown for them, as well as boxing and wrestling events. Upon the resumption of peace, the entertainment provided on the pier continued to principally consist of roller skating, novelty shows, dancing and bands. A new novelty show was Captain Sidney Lawson Smith, who descended from the pier to the seabed in full diving gear and gave a description of what he found. He also took up challenges to find items that had been thrown into the sea.

In the face of competition in the 1920s, the showing of films on the pier declined compared to the established cinemas. However, an increased interest in jazz led to more bands being hired. The roller skating rink was home to the Folkestone Roller Hockey Club, skating games and activities, while amusement machines were introduced by Fred Harrison in a small arcade at the shore end of the pier. The novelty shows continued to draw good crowds with such features as the jolliest face competition, balloon carnivals, the gentleman with the jolliest laugh, best hair for men, the curliest hair, ladies with the sweetest smile, the prettiest children, the most sparkling eyes and even a complexion show that claimed to be the first of its kind in England – all before Butlins! The racy ankle shows, in particular, were very well attended, each contestant having to walk along a bridge leading to the centre of the pavilion, which was screened so only legs up to the knee were visible. The pier was always a very popular vantage point on annual regatta days, and hosted a big carnival with fireworks to round off the day.

Since 1919, the Victoria Pier Syndicate had been very much a family company. Following the resignation of Lloyd in March 1930, the four members of the syndicate consisted of Robert, his wife Edith, and sons Hugh and Joseph. Sadly, in 1934, Robert Forsyth passed away and his

Victoria Pier Syndicate was wound up by Edith, between May and October 1935. By this time, the condition of the pier was causing concern. An inspection revealed that much of the ironwork was corroded and the wooden decking rotten. Nevertheless, Lloyd Forsyth and his Southern Trading Corporation leased the pier until 1937 after which the Ramsgate amusement entrepreneur Dennis Franklin Warren took over. Warren unveiled ambitious plans to totally rebuild the pier entrance with an art deco-styled concrete building containing an entertainment hall, sun lounge, restaurant and bars. However, the plan never came to fruition, nor did Warren's proposal to purchase the pier from the Folkestone Pier & Lift Company, which now consisted of a few elderly directors who lacked the drive and enthusiasm to make the pier profitable.

The pier was closed at the outbreak of the Second World War, but it was subsequently re-opened for a short period. However, visitors were few, as recorded on Tuesday 16 April 1940 when only seven customers paid to use the pier! Two months later, on 11 June, the pier was closed again to allow the centre section of the structure to be blown up as a defence measure. The gap was closed with a small bridge in 1943 when a pump was housed in the pavilion to enable seawater to be used in fighting fires caused by enemy action.

Not surprisingly, the pier became rundown as the war dragged on, and as military restrictions began to be lifted, dare-devil locals and military personnel clambered along it, in spite of the lack of wooden decking. Sadly, one of the intruders deliberately set fire to the Pier Pavilion on Whit Sunday 20 May 1945 and completely destroyed the sea end of the structure.

The fire dashed all hopes that the pier could be repaired and it forlornly lay derelict as arguments raged on as to who should pay for its demolition. The Folkestone Pier & Lift Company had virtually ceased to exist, but nevertheless was summoned on 21 June 1949 for failing to exhibit warning lights on the derelict structure. In the end, it was left to the local landowner, the Earl of Radnor, to commence demolition of the pier in 1952. The last section of the old pier was finally blown up in November 1954. The pier's publican's licence, suspended since 1943, was moved to the Beach Hotel, 4-5 Marine Crescent on 25 May 1955. Today, only the abutment to the pier and a small section of iron supporting column survive to show where it once stood.

15

THE PIERS THAT NEVER WERE

For every pier that was built in the 'Mania' years of 1860-1910, there was another that never got off the ground. Such was the demand to build piers. It appears that almost every watering place at one time had plans to construct a pier, yet many, particularly the smaller resorts, were to remain pierless from lack of finances, local opposition or just plain indifference which scuppered their plans for a 'walk over the water'. Listed below is Kent's 'Piers That Never Were'.

Birchington Epple Bay

Coal was landed here, and in 1891 a pier was envisaged 'where steamers may land'.

Broadstairs

A pier was first proposed in 1879, as reported in the *East Coast Times* in June: 'The formation of the Pier and Hotel Company has been formed for the purpose of building an iron pier or jetty near the Louisa Bridge cutting, and for the purchase of a new hotel now in the course of erection nearby.'

In 1882, another scheme proposed building a 1,200ft pier, south-east from Louisa Gap. In 1903, another application for a pier was made, and on 13 January 1904 the *East Kent Times* reported:

> The proposed new pier at Broadstairs is opposed by Broadstairs & St Peters UDC on the grounds it would be detrimental to the interests of the district, in as much as it was intended to afford facilities for the landing at Broadstairs of a class of excursionists whom it was not desirable to encourage; that the scheme proposed is calculated, by interference with the tides, to divert the flow of sand from Broadstairs beach; that the scheme is calculated to cause the foundation of a sand bar across the entrance to Broadstairs Harbour, and thus to impede the entrance into it of barges and other craft; and that it would destroy the amenities of the Victoria Pleasure Gardens.

The application was refused by the Board of Trade in April 1904.

Cliftonville

In 1893, a development was proposed between the Cliftonville Hotel and Hodges Flagstaff to include a pier, baths, hotels, church and school. However, nothing materialised.

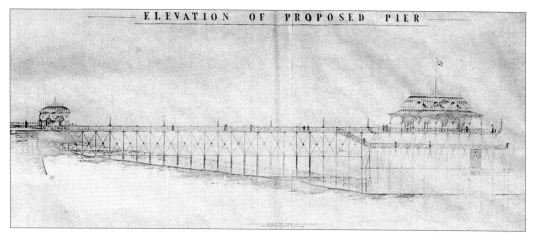

The pier proposed by Hythe in 1887 to commemorate Queen Victoria's Golden Jubilee. *Marlinova Collection*

The plans for the proposed pier at Littlestone-on-Sea, dated 5 October 1889. *Marlinova Collection*

Hythe

The idea for a pier was suggested by Mayor Dan West in 1887 as a memorial to Queen Victoria's Golden Jubilee. The pier was to project out from Princes Parade as part of a development of wide streets and elegant squares. Princes Parade ran from Hythe through Seabrook, to the Sandgate boundary. The South Eastern Railway, which owned the Seabrook (later Imperial) Hotel at the Hythe end of the parade, was to contribute towards the cost of the 250ft pier, which also provided an ornate pavilion. Sadly, none of the proposals were carried out.

Littlestone-on-Sea

The pier was planned as part of the resort development by H.T. Tubbs. His Littlestone Improvement Company erected an ornate water tower (which still survives today), as well as the Marine Parade and Grand Hotel, but the pier did not materialise. However, plans for the grand structure can still be seen in New Romney Town Hall.

Minster-on-Sea

A 7,000ft pier, proposed around 1907, gained approval by the Board of Trade but was never built.

Sandgate

According to Pamela Thompson in *Folkestone – Specious and Gruesome*, Councillor John Jones, a prominent local businessman, applied for permission to build a pier in the early 1900s but was refused by the local council.

Sheerness Banks Town

Sir Edward Banks acquired land in Sheerness in the early years of the nineteenth century with the intention of designing an elegant seaside resort. He laid out Edward Street (later the Broadway in 1827) and built himself a fine mansion on 3 acres of land. Banks Terrace was also erected, and a pier proposed, but local opposition by the Oyster Fisheries Commission, and others, thwarted the plan. Banks' land was eventually sold, and where the grand seaside houses were planned, back-to-back terrace houses were built instead.

Westgate-on-Sea

The *East Coast Times* of 27 March 1879 reported a proposal to erect a 3,000ft pier at this quiet Kentish resort. Nothing further was heard of the scheme, but in 1883 there was a proposal to move the failed iron promenade pier at Ramsgate to Westgate. However, this also never took place.

BIBLIOGRAPHY AND REFERENCES

River Thames Piers

Erith www.bexley.gov.uk
Dartford www.ox.ac.uk
Payne, Francine, *Joyce Green and the River Hospitals* (Author 2001)
Burne, Dr John, *Dartford's Capital River* (Barracuda 1989)
Greenhithe www.greenhithe.co.uk
The Prospectus of the Greenhithe Pier Company

Gravesend

Hilton, John, *Star and Diamond: An Account of Steamboat Competition* (Bygone Kent Vol. 19 Nos. 9 & 10 1998)
Mansfield, F.A., *The History of Gravesend* (Rochester Press 1981)
Ormston, John M., *The Five Minute Crossing: The Tilbury-Gravesend Ferries* (Thurrock Local History Society 1998)
Gravesend Chronology 56AD-2000 (Towncentric 2001)
Benson, James, revised by Hiscock, Robert Heath *A History of Gravesend* (Phillimore 1981)
Historic Gravesham, No. 49 (Gravesend Historical Society 2003)

River Medway Piers

www.medwaypilots.com
Hart, Brian, *The Hundred of Hoo Railway* (Wild Swan Publications 1989)
MacDougall, Philip, *The Hoo Peninsula* (John Hallewell Publications 1980)
Foweraker, Lewis, *Upnor – A Village History* (Author 2000)
Moss, Alan and Russell, Kevin, *Rochester in old picture postcards* (European Library 1988)
MacDougall, Philip, *Old Chatham* (Meresborough Books 1983)
Baldwin, Ronald A., *The Gillingham Chronicles* (Baggins Book Bazaar 1998)
Eastleigh, Robert L., *Queenborough Pier and the Flushing Ferry* (Bygone Kent Vol. 7 No. 3 1986)
Gray, Adrian, *The London, Chatham & Dover Railway* (Meresborough Books 1984)

Sheerness

Eastleigh, Robert L., *Sheerness Pier* (Bygone Kent Vol. 7 No. 1 1986)
Eastleigh, Robert L., *Sheerness Pier* (Piers Information Bureau Sheet No. 1 1989)
East Kent Gazette & Times 27-1-86

Tankerton

West, Douglas, *Portrait of a Seaside Town: Historic Photographs of Whitstable* (Author 1984)
West, Douglas, *Third Portrait of a Seaside Town; Historic Photographs of Whitstable* (Author 1988)

Herne Bay and Hampton-on-Sea

Mount, Frank, *My Recollections of Hampton* (Author 1942)
Coulson, L.H., *A Chronology of Herne Bay to 1913* (Kent County Library 1984)
Pout, Roger, *The Early Years of Roller Hockey* (Author 1993)
Hawkins, John, *Herne Bay in Old Photographs* (Alan Sutton 1991)
Hawkins, John, *Herne Bay Revisited* (Alan Sutton 1999)
Gough, Harold, *A Picture Book of Herne Bay* (Meresborough Books 1983)
Gough, Harold, *Herne Bay's Piers* (Pier Head Publications 2002)
Turner, Roger, *Hook, Line & Sinker: A History of the Herne Bay Angling Association* (Herne Bay Angling
    Association 2004)
Kitching, Lester, *Herne Bay Pier* (Piers Information Bureau Sheet No. 3 1989)
Turner, Keith, *Pier Railways & Tramways of the British Isles* (Oakwood Press 1999)
MacDougall, Philip, *Three Piers for Herne Bay* (Bygone Kent Vol. 5 No. 10 1984)
Gough, Harold, *Captain Gardiner: Herne Bay's Staunch Piermaster 1844-1862* (Bygone Kent Vol. 6 No. 9
    1985)
G.E. Baddeley, *The Tramways of Kent,* Vol. 2 (Light Railway Transport League 1975)
Herne Bay Press (various issues)
National Archives BT31/3203/18656
National Archives MT10/1261
National Archives CRES58/462
National Archives MT6/1318/3
National Archives MT10/661
National Archives MT10/1202

Margate

Bygone Margate (The Journal of the Margate Historical Society, various issues)
East Kent Times (various issues)
Easdown, Martin, *Margate Jetty* (Piers Information Bureau Sheet No. 16 1989)
Bailey, Ivor, *Piering into the Past* (Bygone Kent Vol. 1 No. 1 1980)

Broadstairs

Simmonds, Bob, *Broadstairs Harbour* (Michael's Bookshop 2006)

Ramsgate

Easdown, Martin, *A Fateful Finger of Iron* (Michael's Bookshop 2006)

Pegwell Bay

Easdown, Martin, *Adventures in Shrimpville or Pegwell Bay as a Seaside Resort 1760-1916* (Marlinova 2005, revised and reprinted by Michael's Bookshop 2006)

Deal

Easdown, Martin, *Deal Pier: A Concrete Masterpiece?* (Piers – The Journal of the National Piers Society, No. 42 Winter, 1996/97)
Collyer, David G., *The Day the Nora went through the Pier* (Bygone Kent, Vol. 13 No. 9, 1992)
Holyoake, Gregory, *Old Deal & Walmer* (Meresborough Books 1991)
East Kent Mercury (various issues)
Easdown, Martin and Eastleigh, Robert L., *Deal Pier* (Piers Information Bureau Sheet, No. 12, 1989)
Holyoake, Gregory, *Deal: Sad Smuggling Town* (S.P. Publications 2001)
Holyoake, Gregory, *Three Deal Piers* (Bygone Kent, Vol. 2 No. 7, 1981)

Dover

Easdown, Martin, *Dover Promenade Pier* (Piers Information Bureau Sheet, No. 8, 1989)
MacDougall, Philip, *Dover's Short-lived Pleasure Pier* (Bygone Kent, Vol. 7 No. 12, 1986)
Dover Express (various issues)
The History of Dover Harbour
National Archives BT31/1591/5282
National Archives BT31/4354/28279

Folkestone

Victoria's Golden Pier by Martin Easdown (Marlin Publications 1998)
National Archives BT31/31967/92765
National Archives BT31/2078/9237
National Archives BT297/782

The Piers that never were

Easdown, Martin, *The Piers that never were* (Piers – The Journal of the National Piers Society, No. 63, Spring 2002)

General Pier and Seaside related books

Adamson, Simon, *Seaside Piers* (Batsford 1977)
Mickleburgh, Timothy J., *The Guide to British Piers 2nd Edition* (Piers Information Bureau 1988)
Bainbridge, Cyril, *Pavilions on the Sea* (Robert Hale 1986)
Easdown, Martin and Riding, Richard, *A Guide to Collecting Seaside Pier Postcards* (Authors 2006)
Whyman, John, *The Early Kentish Seaside* (Alan Sutton/Kent Archives Office 1985)
Stafford, Felicity and Yates, Nigel, *The Later Kentish Seaside* (Alan Sutton/Kent Archives Office 1985)

Other local titles published by Tempus

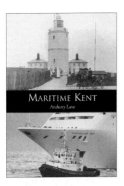

Maritime Kent

ANTHONY LANE

Kent has a long coastline and this, together with its position as the English county closest to Europe, has meant that it has a long history of seafaring. It also has a long record of facing attack from hostile shores. This book describes the county's maritime history over the last 200 years. The many photographs show how the ships have changed, and how the lives of the mariners have altered.

978-0-7524-1769-1

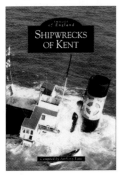

Shipwrecks of Kent

ANTHONY LANE

Kent has witnessed the passing of ships since the beginning of recorded history. The Romans landed there, and armed vessels from Spain, Holland, France and Germany have threatened its shores. This book provides a reminder of many of the more famous wrecks in the area, and includes some not so familiar disasters from the past and describes some strange coincidences that have occurred over the last two centuries.

978-0-7524-1720-2

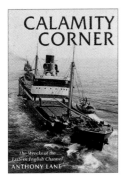

Calamity Corner: The Wrecks of the Eastern English Channel

ANTHONY LANE

For over five centuries, the English Channel's eastern approaches have seen more shipwrecks than almost any other part of the coastline. Well known for its shifting sands, narrow sea lanes and rapidly changing weather patterns, Calamity Corner illustrates just how treacherous this stretch of coast can be.

978-0-7524-3163-5

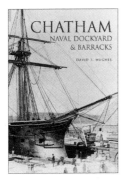

Chatham Naval Dockyard

DAVID HUGHES

This fascinating volume of photographs and ephemera on the Chatham Naval Dockyard and Barracks looks at this historic institution from its early days through its role in more recent years, through the First and Second World Wars to the Falklands campaign.

978-0-7524-3248-9

If you are interested in purchasing other books published by Tempus, or in case you have difficulty finding any Tempus books in your local bookshop, you can also place orders directly through our website

www.tempus-publishing.com